A Guide To

INTERVIEWING
SEX CRIME VICTIMS

"Getting It Right!"

By

Don Howell and Susan Davidson Dalberg

LawTech Publishing Co., Ltd.

A Guide To
INTERVIEWING SEX CRIME VICTIMS
"Getting It Right!"

Copyright© 1999 by Detective Don Howell
and Susan Davidson Dalberg

QWIK-CODE is a trademark of **LawTech Publishing Co., Ltd.**

LawTech Publishing Co., Ltd.
1060 Calle Cordillera, Ste. 105
San Clemente, CA 92673

(949) 498-4815
Fax: (949) 498-4858
e-mail: lawtech@fea.net
Web site: www.lawtech-pub.com

See outside back cover for product information.

Comments and suggestions are welcome.

p: 208

Printed in the United States of America

ISBN: 0-915905-92-2

ACKNOWLEDGMENTS

This book is dedicated to Marie Baxter and all of the others from whom we have learned so much.

Appreciation is extended to Doreen Weaver, Paul Howell and Marilyn Droz for their technical assistance in the production of this handbook.

Our sincere thanks to Randy Niznik, Probation Officer and instructor for the Criminal Justice Program at Santa Ana College, for requesting this book as a resource for law enforcement, social workers, therapists and anyone working with children. Most especially, we are appreciative of his confidence that we were the most qualified to put it together.

"When the words *Justice* and *Juvenile* are synonymous, the scales will be balanced and we will have accomplished our mission."

Don Howell/Susan Dalberg

ABOUT THE AUTHORS

A California native, Don Howell graduated with honors from California State University at Los Angeles with a Bachelor of Science Degree in Police Science and Administration. He has spent the last twenty five years as a police officer for two different Southern California cities. Don has been a detective for over fifteen years, specializing in the investigation of sexual assaults and child abuse. He is a court certified expert in these areas and is a highly sought after consultant to other agencies in complex cases.

As a consultant to the California Commission on Police Officers Standards and Training, Don was considered to be one of the best in his field and was selected to assist in making a telecourse regarding rape investigations.

He is a long time member of the California Sexual Assault Investigators' Association, and was the Child Sexual Abuse Network's (CSAN) "Detective of the Year" in 1990. In spite of his busy schedule, Don still finds time to teach at police academies and community colleges. Don is a founding board member of the California branch of the National Center for Missing and Exploited Children.

Known for his professional talent, wit, keen eye and instinct, Don offers valuable advice to any law enforcement officer or social worker faced with interviewing children.

Along with longtime friend and child advocate, Susan Davidson Dalberg, Don joined forces to write a simple, easy to understand handbook on interviewing sexual assault victims, emphasizing the tools needed to talk to kids under eight years of age.

* * * *

Susan Davidson Dalberg graduated from the University of Oklahoma. Subsequently, Susan has received over 3,000 hours in training specifically addressing the issues of victimization—the victims, system and the perpetrators. In 1981, dealing with the residual effects of her own abuse as a child, Susan started an advocacy center for victims of abuse, exploitation and kidnapping. That advocacy center ultimately became the Adam Walsh Child Resource Center, now the National Center for Missing and Exploited Children, California Branch. Her primary involvement entailed working with victims exposed to the law enforcement and court community and a commitment to educate and to change the system.

Susan has lectured and continues to guest lecture at police academies, community colleges and universities. She has received numerous local, state and federal recognition awards for her work on behalf of children and victims.

Currently, Susan is working on her Doctorate in Clinical Hypnotherapy, her goal being to minimize the trauma to victims as they remember their painful experience.

Together, she and Don bring over forty years of experience and dedication to children into this textbook. It is their hope that all students will benefit from their combined early years of stumbling (when there was little, if any, knowledge about this subject) and derive a level of confidence by utilizing these two individuals' expertise, insight and opinions on how to work with victims.

FORWARD

This book is long overdue and certainly the two authors, with whom I am personally acquainted, are the individuals with the experience and passion to present it in such a non-threatening, easy to implement, system and style. As the host of *America's Most Wanted*, I see first hand the lack of information available on interviewing victims, primarily children, in a way that is effective and non-traumatic. By implementing such a simple system described by Howell and Davidson Dalberg, perhaps the statistics of the crime of child sexual abuse and rape by repeated offenders can be drastically reduced.

John Walsh
Host
America's Most Wanted

TABLE OF CONTENTS

CHAPTER 1 - GET IT RIGHT! GET IT ALL! GET IT THE FIRST TIME! 3
  Interview Reports and California Penal Code Section 293 5

CHAPTER 2 - INTERVIEWING CHILDREN AGES 2 - 7 7
  Background Information 8
  First Contact with the Child Using The Stick Figure System (SFS) 9
  Physical Setting for the Interview 10
  Rapport Building 11
  Identifying Body Parts 11
  Pre-Drawn Anatomy 13
  Use of Anatomically Correct Dolls 14
  Good Touch vs. Bad Touch 14
  Qualifying as a Witness 14
  Attention Span 15
  Number of Counts 16
  Time Frames 17
  Secrets 17
  Other Victims 17
  Doing it Correctly 18
  Interview of Child 2-7 Years Using The Stick Figure System 18
  False Reports 23
  Repeating Questions 25
  Tape-Recording / Video-Taping 25
  Teaming with Social Services 27
  Protective Custody 27
  ASAV: Alleged Sexual Assault Victim Examination 39
  Interviews at School 41
  Cross-reporting to the Child Abuse Registry 42
  Photographs as Evidence 43
  Report Narrative: 2-7 Year-old Victim 43

CHAPTER 3 - INTERVIEWING CHILDREN AGES 8 - 12 47
  Background 47
  Seating Arrangement 47
  Terminology 47
  Teaming with Social Services 48
  Out-Of-Home Suspect 48
  Victim / Suspect Profile 48
  Victim Gender 49
  Family Dynamics 49
  Number of Counts 50
  Attention Span 50
  Qualifying as a Witness 50
  Fixated Pedophile 51
  Regressed Pedophile 51
  Other Types of Molesters 51
  Discussion 52
  Cross Reporting 52

Number of Counts 53
False Reports. 54
Interview— 8-12 Year Old Victim 54
    Report Narrative: 8- 12 Year Old Victim 55
CHAPTER 4 - INTERVIEWING AGES 13 - 18 59
Background Information. 59
First Contact with the Victim 59
Building Rapport with a Teen 60
Manipulation by Victims 60
    Sample Narrative: Manipulative Teenage Victim. 61
Male Perpetrator/ Male Victim 64
Male Perpetrator / Female Victim 66
Incest 66
    Report Narrative: Incest Victim 68
Female Perpetrators - Female Victims 72
Female Perpetrators - Male Victims 73
Example: Adult Female Perpetrator - Adolescent Male Victim. 75
Clandestine Telephone Calls From Victims 77
Date Rape 77
Sex of Interviewer 78
Stranger Rape 78
Medical Exams 78
False Reports. 79
CHAPTER 5 - INTERVIEWING AGES 18 - 80 81
When The Suspect Is A Stranger 81
    First contact. 81
    Stalking 81
    Predator Rapist 82
    Modus Operandi vs. Fantasy of Rapist 84
    Sexual Assault Phases 85
    Age of Victim. 86
    Perpetrator's Rape Kits 87
    Rape Trauma Syndrome 88
Interview: Rape Victim. 88
    Male vs. Female Interviewers 93
    False Rape Reports 94
    Rape Reports: Making it "Better Than it is". 99
    Report Narrative: Stranger Rape 99
Date Rape / Acquaintance Rape 104
    Report Narrative: Date / Acquaintance Rape 105
Spousal Rape. 108
    Ongoing Spousal Abuse. 109
    Report Narrative: Ongoing Spousal Rape. 109
    Estranged Husband 111
    Report Narrative: Estranged Husband Spousal Rape. 112
Senile / Elderly Victims. 114
    Report Narrative: Senile / Elderly Victim 115

Conditional Exam / Interview...116
Mentally Handicapped / Retarded Victims 117
  Background Information 118
  Interview: Mentally Handicapped / Retarded Victim 118
  Report Narrative: Mentally Handicapped / Retarded Victim Report...119
Satanic Cults 121
Unlawful Intercourse 125
  Report Narrative: Unlawful Intercourse 126
To Tape or Not to Tape 127
When the Victim Won't Talk...128
Female Anatomy 129
Teaming Officers and Advocates 130

CHAPTER 6 - THE ADVOCATE'S PERSPECTIVE.................135
Child Victims: "Potholes in the Road That Leads to Justice" 136
  Strength Through Association..................................136
  Marie's Story...137
  Statements You Don't Want to Hear - or Make 139
  Case Study: "Little Bit"..139
  Ignorance Is Not Bliss! 144
  Case Study: Sherrie..144
  Is it the Truth, a Lie, a Fib or a False Memory? 145
  Law Enforcement / Advocate Teaming Benefits 147
  Case Study: Multiple Offenders / Multiple Victims, "Day-care" 148
  Brainwashing a Child..151
  The Tape Recording Issue 152
  "Who Told You What to Say?" 153
  Rush to Judgment..154

CHAPTER 7 - ODDS & ENDS OF "BUTTING IN" 159
Child Abuse Reporting 159
  Case Study: Unfounded..162
The Accommodation Syndrome..164
Satanic Cult Victimization..164
Strength Through Association 165

CHAPTER 8 - ADVOCACY FOR ADULT VICTIMS.....................167
The Role of the Adult Advocate...167
  Case Study: Kathy..168

CHAPTER 9 - THE MOBILE MOLESTER / SEX CRIME PERPETRATOR...171

CHAPTER 10 - DOMESTIC VIOLENCE 173
Spousal Abuse - Extra Protection.......................................173

CHAPTER 11 - ADVOCATES WANTED-LOW PAY, LONG HOURS 177
Using Advocates to Defuse an Explosive Situation. 179
Finding an Advocate to "Team With" 180

CHAPTER 12 - PROFOUND SILENCE 181

EPILOGUE 183

APPENDIX A - Rape Trauma Syndrome 185

TABLE OF CONTENTS

**APPENDIX B - Indicators of False Allegations
of Sexual Assault By Strangers** 188

APPENDIX C- Stick Figure System 191

BIBLIOGRAPHY 193

LIST OF ILLUSTRATIONS. 196

WE'D LIKE TO HEAR FROM YOU!! 197

INTRODUCTION

This text introduces a unique approach to the art of interviewing sex crimes victims of all ages. This new concept of combining the skills of the police officer with those of the victim's advocate creates an advanced form of teamwork. This team approach enhances the skills of the investigator in obtaining essential information while providing much needed support for the victims.

For too long, there has existed a void of information on how to interview victims of sex crimes. One can find countless reference materials on interviewing perpetrators of assault, burglary or car theft. How to take a stolen vehicle report has countless instructional pieces. However, in the arena of sexual abuse, there have been only treatment and survivor pieces written, none of which "cut to the bottom line" and give police, social workers or legal advocates the tools to do the initial interview which result in:

(a) The comfort of the victim

(b) The ability of the interviewer to get all of the information

(c) The steps to take cases to prosecution when possible

This textbook fills that critical void.

The instructions and examples in this book will give even the novice an "A B C" or "by-the-numbers" approach to interviewing children. Following these steps will get you started and take you through to the end. It will tell you what to do at the very first contact with the child, where to sit, what to say, and how to close the interview.

The Stick Figure System (SFS) is a method that works with very young children. It provides a framework to work within, which enables the interviewer and the child to work together to have a "conversation" about the alleged molestation instead of an awkward question and answer session. By creating simple drawings together, the investigator and the child victim can build rapport and establish the elements of the crime. These steps vary with the age of the child, but are vital to every case.

When dealing with older children and adult victims, some of the steps may be skipped, but the officer will learn the appropriate techniques and demeanor for dealing with adults that parallels the basic method used with children. All of this information is the foundation for interviewing *anyone* who has been the victim of any crime. By following this simple technique for interviewing victims, and adding some of your own personal creativity, you should have all the tools you need to handle almost any of these situations. These proven techniques, applied within the framework of the officer-advocate partnership, will dramatically improve your results.

It's impossible to cite the laws of each state as they relate to the investigation and prosecution of sexual abuse. Although we have included examples of California statutes and regulations throughout the text, the reader should carefully research their appropriate state laws and case decisions.

There will always be an offender out there who will do something so totally bizarre it denies any logic or preconceived idea as to what sex offenders *normally* do. In sex crimes, almost every situation has some new twist or turn. The saying "just when you think you've heard it all," is especially true for sex crimes.

If you get stuck and need help, we are only a phone call away.

SECTION 1
A LAW ENFORCEMENT PERSPECTIVE

THIS PAGE INTENTIONALLY LEFT BLANK

CHAPTER 1

GET IT RIGHT! GET IT ALL! GET IT THE FIRST TIME!

This text is designed to help you do the above three critical things. It is specifically designed for interviewing sexual assault victims, primarily children. Having been a police officer for over twenty-five years, I know that most officers would rather be involved in a shooting with a band of bank robbers as opposed to interviewing a five-year old who has been fondled by a neighbor. This fear of interviewing children is due to a lack of a plan, or method, about what to actually ask and how to go about asking it. In reality, the younger the child is, the easier it is to interview them, because children of this age have no prejudices, predilections, or preconceived ideas about the actual events which took place. All you need is basic knowledge about how children think, then how to establish a connection between you and the child so that he or she will tell you what you need to know. With a few, simple techniques and procedures, you will be able to *get it right, get it all, and get it the first time.*

While this handbook is written from a law enforcement and advocacy perspective, the technique, system and principles contained herein can be used by police officers, social workers, therapists, teachers, lawyers or anyone who needs to obtain factual information from a child and prepare a report.

As children get older they become more verbal, which obviously makes communicating with them somewhat easier, but the dynamics of the molestation itself becomes more complex. Fortunately, with a little background as to how and why these crimes occur, you will know what to look for and what questions to ask.

Teenagers and adults present a different set of problems for the interviewer. However, these can also be easily overcome once you have an idea of what to expect and how to present yourself to the victim.

This text will focus mainly on talking to people who have been the victims of some type of sex crime. However, the same principles can apply to victims who have been physically abused, neglected, emotionally abused, and/or have been witnesses to non-sexual crimes, such as robbery, assault, spousal abuse or any other type of criminal activity.

This book is designed to give the novice a starting point as to how to begin the conversation with a sexual assault victim and will also help experienced interviewers fine tune their skills. If you already have some sort of a technique or a style that you use when interviewing children and other victims which is successful for you, by all means continue to use it. Please feel free to add any of this information to the techniques you are already using.

In my experience, I have found that using the methods described here will get you the information needed in about 95% of the cases you encounter.

Sex offenders vary widely in their motivations, psychological dynamics, the fantasies they create for themselves, and in the way they approach and assault both children and adults. This book is not intended to try to describe the various types of sex offenders, but rather is designed to assist you in the *most likely* type of situation in which you will find yourself. If material you read in this text at times appears to be contradictory, it is only because of the sometimes overlapping profiles of offenders, *not* a mistake in the text. (There are numerous texts describing sexual offenders listed in the bibliography in the back of this book.)

This book is written as a starting place for the interview process of the victims of these crimes. Most of the text is broken into general age ranges of victims of sexual assault. These age ranges are approximate only, and are merely guidelines to follow during the course of your contacts with the victims.

Interview Reports and California Penal Code Section 293

Recently, there was a change in California law to help protect the identity of sexual assault victims. (Penal Code Sec. 293 - see your individual state laws.) This change in the law requires that law enforcement personnel conceal the name, address, etc. of all sexual assault victims so that the suspects cannot gain access to this information. Because of this change in the law, most law enforcement agencies have initiated a protocol for protecting the identity of the victim and have implemented systems in which a confidential number is assigned to each victim, such as "97-123." For that reason, in the dialog/narrative portions of this text, victims are identified using numbers rather than their full names

However, in cases involving "in-family" types of molestation and/or sexual assault in which all of the participants are already known to each other, and where there are multiple victims, I assign a confidential number to the primary victim and, when listing that number on the crime report face sheet, in the "victim" portion, list the number and the first name of the victim; i.e., "97-123-Bill." This way the report complies with PC 293 since it does not divulge dates of birth and addresses, etc. of these victims, yet aids the officer in being able to quickly identify the source of the information and to distinguish between victims.

THIS PAGE INTENTIONALLY LEFT BLANK

CHAPTER 2

INTERVIEWING CHILDREN
AGES 2 - 7

It is possible to obtain a great deal of information from a very young child, regardless of their limited verbal skills. When it comes to interviewing very young child victims, the techniques are basically the same as when interviewing older children with minor variations due to their age. When dealing with a two-year-old, however, the attention span is obviously much shorter, so they will require more frequent breaks during the interview process than older children. However, building a criminal case based solely on the statements of a child this young is almost impossible. If a child has had preschool education and/or is very mature for his/her age, you can obviously gain more information. Nonetheless, a young child's ability to qualify as a witness is always limited.

Any successful criminal prosecution is going to be based primarily on witness statements and physical evidence. Identifying and interviewing witnesses who may have actually observed the molestation or taken some spontaneous statements from the child and/or suspect are very important to document. Additionally, the medical examination by trained personnel will be very important in establishing the elements of the crime.

Children who have been molested may give many nonverbal clues that *something traumatic* has happened to them. For example, a child that has been toilet-trained may regress to wetting the bed. They might begin having severe and repeated nightmares or may line up their stuffed animals around their bed or at the bedroom door as symbolic defenders in an attempt to keep the offender away. They may refuse to go to a baby-sitter or a relative's house where they had enjoyed going to in the past.

Caution should be used and no rush to judgments made solely on the existence of any of these activities. None of these behaviors in and of themselves prove that a child has been molested. There may be other reasons for these behaviors. The investigating officer should question the family of the child to determine whether or not any of these behavior changes have been noted by the family members, when they occurred, what statements the child has made, if any, during the behavior and include that information in their report.

Background Information

I have never interviewed a child without having some background as to what allegedly had taken place. This information usually comes from the parent, school teacher, nurse, doctor, social worker, or somebody who has already had some contact with the child. Typically, the child will have disclosed some information to one of these individuals before you would be notified. It may be as simple as the child having told their teacher that the stepfather has been touching their "private places" at bath time. This type of information gives you a very valuable head start. The suspect has been identified, and the information given to the secondary person by the child has given you an idea as to the extent of the molestation.

A more typical source of background information is when a parent brings a child in for an interview. In this case, the child has told the parent about the victimization and you will have a better picture of the extent of the molestation, including the identity of the actual suspect. Such information as the name of the perpetrator, their age, address, physical description, etc. can be gained from the adult who gives you this background information.

While this is valuable information, you have to be careful not to lead the victim through the interview based on the statements given to you by other parties. Since the person obtaining the background information is not skilled or trained in interviewing children with regard to sexual assault, they frequently added their interpretation as to what the child is saying to the description they are giving to you. It is doubtful that the person getting the background information will have clarified with the child such issues as whether or not the touching was over the clothing or skin-to-skin, or if it occurred once or multiple times.

I prefer to interview the adult AFTER I have spoken with the child for two reasons. First, it makes the interview with the child "cleaner," eliminating the perception that I led the child through the interview based on the history given by the adult. Second, when I "get it all" from the child, it eliminates the need to obtain a detailed (hearsay) statement from the adult. In this situation, the initial overview/background statement from the adult is all that is needed. (The exception to this would be a fresh complaint statement made by the child, which is discussed later.)

First Contact with the Child Using The Stick Figure System (SFS)

Children ages 2-7 accept the world as it is presented to them. There is really no need to go through any lengthy introductions explaining who you are or why you are there to talk with the child. This information is usually too complex for the child to understand, and wastes valuable time. It is more important to make an immediate contact with the child so that the rapport building process can take place, thus not wasting any of the limited amount of minutes you have to speak with the child.

This is best done by giving the kid a "high five" as soon as you make contact. Every child I have ever spoken to (over 1,000) understands the concept of giving someone a "high five." If they don't, it's a very simple thing to teach them.

The next thing you ask is, "How old are you?" No matter what their response is, you always tell them that they look "much bigger than the average kid that age." For psychological reasons, children like to think they are larger (or smarter, or prettier, or faster) than others of their same age. I simply reinforce that needed perception in my statement and give them some additional self-confidence.

You can also ask them if they attend preschool. The preschool information can be very valuable to you as to how easy it will be to establish future rapport with the child. Every kid who has been in preschool has done a lot of drawing and learning activities generated around working in a one-on-one situation with an adult.

Physical Setting for the Interview

My experience has shown that the dinner table is the best place to conduct such an interview. In most households, the dinner table is not only where meals are served, but it is where most family business is conducted. It gives you a place to sit and a table to use for writing notes. The child is comfortable sitting at the dinner table and this is a natural environment for them to sit and talk to adults.

Contrary to popular belief, "child-friendly environments" really do not assist in producing a lot of factual information for a police report. Child-friendly environments are very good for conducting therapy or for school settings, but when it comes to conducting a factual "what happened" type of interview, the kitchen table is the best location for a comfortable discussion.

Do not have the child sitting *across* the table from you when you conduct the interview. It creates an artificial barrier between you and the child. *Instead, sit at the corner of the table.* If you are right-handed, sit with the child at 90 degrees from you on your left side. This allows you to write and draw with the child without your arm blocking the child's view of what you are doing. Left-handed? Simply reverse the seating, staying at the corners of the table. (Refer to Illustration # 1, page 29.)

Don't be afraid to sit close to the child, or be concerned if the child wants to touch your uniform. They are naturally curious at this age and simple touching won't hurt your uniform. If you are successful in making a good connection with the child, by the end of the interview, the child may be sitting in your lap helping you draw while discussing the actual molestation allegations.

If the child wants a parent present during the interview, that is acceptable. However, be sure to limit it to only one parent, and also try to keep other children and family members from interrupting the interview process.

Rapport Building

This is accomplished very simply. Take any piece of standard size paper, such as the continuation page for a crime report, or the diagram page from a traffic accident report or any other paper that allows you enough blank space on which to draw. You can then begin to engage the child in a "comfort building" activity.

Ask the child if he or she knows how to "trace hands." If the child has been in preschool, they have done this many times in the past; if not, it's an easy thing to teach. *You* first trace one hand of the child by putting their hand on the piece of paper and using your pen to outline their fingers. Next, have the child outline your hand on the same piece of paper. If the child is very young, you may have to help them actually hold the pen as they trace your fingers. These drawings may be a bit crude, but they are not intended for museum submission. They are simply great bonding exercises. The drawing may be left with the child to display on the refrigerator when you leave, or you may discard them (out of the child's presence) after the end of the interview. Whatever the ultimate fate of the drawings, the exercise develops a bond and begins of the process of you and the child *working together.* (Refer to Illustration # 2, page 30.)

Identifying Body Parts

Now that you have established a rapport with the child using the hand tracing exercises, you are ready to move on to the identification of body parts using a more refined drawing exercise. Because of vocabulary limitations of a child of this age, you need to establish that you are talking the same language when it comes to identifying physical anatomy. This is done quite easily by drawing a stick figure on another piece of paper incorporating the Stick Figure System which *will* be maintained as evidence. (Refer to Illustration # 3, page 31.)

As you start this process, ask the child, "Can you help me draw a people?" For some reason, the word "people" creates an immediate bond between you and the child. They know you speak their language. Always be sure to use the word, "people" as opposed to "person," "individual," "man" or "woman."

Ask the child if they want to draw a boy or a girl "people." In my experience, the child usually chooses the same sex drawing that they are. You label the piece of paper "girl" (if that is the case) and you begin to draw the stick figure. As you draw a large circle for the head, you tell the child, "I don't draw people very good, so don't laugh at me, okay?" Again, this is a real rapport builder between you and the child and the child is now working with you as you continue the stick figure.

Next, draw a single line down from the circle to represent the body, "Y" shaped lines at the base of the body to indicate the legs, and then two stick arms out to the side.

You now begin the process of working with the child to fill in the stick figure drawing. You start with the top of the drawing and ask the child to identify what else is needed to make the stick figure look like a real "people." You may have to point to the child's nose and ask her what that is in order for her to understand the concept. Once you point to the nose, you draw in the nose and label it on the side of the drawing as "nose." You do the same thing for mouth, ears, eyes, etc. You can also ask the child if they want to make this person happy or sad. If the child wants it to be a happy person, then you make a smiling face; for a sad person, draw a frown.

As you continue down the body, ask the child to identify the hands, elbows, knees, feet, etc. As you do so, you label each of these body parts off to the side as the child gives you the name for them. If the child identifies the hands as being "fingers," then you write down "fingers". If she identifies the feet as being "toes," or "shoes," you write those words.

After you have identified hands, elbows, knees, feet, you go to the area of the navel. In every case I have had, the child has always referred to the navel as a "belly button." After identifying that part of the body, you point to the groin area of the drawing. Normally, the child will immediately respond with whatever they call that part of the body. A girl may refer to this part of the body as her "vagina," "twinkie," "butterfly," "pee-pee" or other such names. Whatever term she uses, write that word to the side of the drawing. If you are interviewing a boy, he will most likely identify the genitals as being his "penis," "wiener," "pee-pee," etc. If the child gives an "X-rated" term for body parts, write that down also, and continue the interviewing process without commenting on the term given for the genitals.

After identifying the genitals, simply turn the paper over quickly and ask the child what would a person have on the back part of their body in that same general area. The child should respond with their "butt," "bottom" or other such term. After determining their term for the buttock area, turn the paper back over and start to identify other parts of the body. At this time, I usually point to the neck or chin or arm, in order to get the child to identify some other body parts so we don't focus in immediately on the genitals.

If you are speaking to a girl, you will want to go back to the genital area and ask the child, "what does a boy have in this area?" Hopefully, the girl will identify a boy's body parts as being his "penis," "wiener" or something similar. The same is true if you are interviewing a boy. Ask him what a girl has in that area, and hopefully, he will respond with something that is a common term used for a girl's genitals.

If the child appears to be reluctant to tell you what the family name is for private parts of their body, it is okay for the parent (who is sitting in on the interview) to prompt the child with that term. The child will translate this into the parent giving permission for them to continue with identifying the rest of their body parts.

Once you have identified the body parts, it is an easy step to start asking about any touching of the genitals, who is doing the touching, and under what circumstances. (The procedure is discussed in the next section.)

Pre-Drawn Anatomy

Some police departments and social service departments have what are called pre-drawn pictures of male and female adults and male and female children. (Refer to Illustration #'s 4 -7, pages 32-35.) Sometimes, they will use the pre-drawns to help identify body parts since they are more lifelike than the stick figure formula. The use of these drawings is fine; however, I have never carried them with me, and I don't think that most police officers would carry them either. Using pre-drawns eliminates the spontaneity of the interaction between the officer and the child. You may lose some very interesting evidentiary type of statements made by the child if they are not interacting with you as completely as they have to do with the stick figure drawing.

Use of Anatomically Correct Dolls

Several years ago, the use of anatomically correct dolls was quite the rage in law enforcement for interviewing children. However, it was found that these dolls were too suggestive since they are the only type of dolls the child would ever see that actually have genitals attached to the body. Because of this, the child has a tendency to focus in on those genitals as opposed to carrying on a conversation with you. Because of that, anatomically correct dolls are rarely used by law enforcement today.

If a child is stumbling over a term for a body part, or simply can't describe what actually happened, you may want to use one of the child's own dolls to give them a tool to describe where the person touched them.

Good Touch vs. Bad Touch

If the child is verbal enough, you might ask them if they know the difference between a good touch and a bad touch. If they aren't sure, you can explain to them that a good touch is something that is caring or comforting, like a hug. A bad touch would be something that is secret, or hurts, or makes them feel uncomfortable. This leads you right into the questioning of the child that asks, "Has anyone ever touched you in a bad way?"

Qualifying as a Witness

The general rule of law is that a witness is considered qualified to testify in court unless there is some information to make the court feel that the witness does not know the difference between the truth and a lie. Sometimes, this will come up in a courtroom setting where someone, usually the defense attorney, will want to know if the child knows or is able to express the difference between telling the truth and telling a lie, or the difference between right and wrong.

In California, the interviewing police officers are now allowed to testify at the preliminary hearing on behalf of the victim. (Proposition 115, Code of Civil Proc. Sec. 872 - See your individual state laws.) You are going to have to be able to tell the court that you established the concept of truth versus non-truth with the witness during the time that you interviewed them. There is a very simple way to do that. Normally, what you do is point at the child's shirt and ask them what color it is. If the shirt is blue, you ask the child, *"If I were to say that the shirt was red, instead of blue, would that be the truth, or would it be a lie?"* Hopefully, the child would respond by saying, *"That would be a lie,"* or, *"That would be silly,"* or *"That would be stupid,"* etc. You then ask the child, *"Are you supposed to tell a lie, or are you supposed to tell the truth?"* The child should respond by saying, *"You're supposed to tell the truth."* You then ask the child, *"What happens when you tell a lie?"* The child should respond by saying, *"I'm put in time-out,"* or *"Mama gets mad at me."* This establishes that the child knows the difference between right and wrong, between telling the truth and a lie, and that there are consequences to telling lies.

Attention Span

The younger the child, the shorter their attention span. I have seen many interviewers work a child far past their ability to concentrate on one particular subject. You, as an interviewer, have to understand the limitations of the child. In very general terms, a child between the ages of four and seven years will have an attention span initially of perhaps four to eight minutes.

After that four-to-eight minute time span, you will notice that the child becomes fidgety and is not concentrating as well as in the beginning. You need to take the child off of the subject of the molestation for approximately forty-five seconds to one minute. Any longer than that, and the child will become too absorbed in the new subject matter and will not want to come back to the subject of the molestation. (There will be further discussion as to how to do this in subsequent sections.)

After this forty-five second to one-minute break from the primary subject, you bring the child back on topic for perhaps two or three more minutes. After the two or three-minute additional interview time, the child will start to show signs of fatigue and it will be necessary for you to take them off subject for approximately another minute or so.

After this second break from the primary interview subject, you will have an opportunity to bring them back on subject for perhaps a minute or two to ask some cleanup type questions before the child's attention span has been lost altogether. If you try to interview the child beyond their attention span, they will begin to talk about things that will be completely out of context of the subject you are talking about. Be sure not to fatigue the child or interview them past their ability to intelligently respond to you.

Number of Counts

During the course of the interview, you will need to try to establish the number of times that a criminal act took place. If the child is very young, you may only get a statement such as, "it happened a few times" versus "it happened a lot of times." The child may be able to say that it happened four or five times. If they give you an exact number, such as "five," ask them to count to five, so you can be sure they understand that concept.

With younger children, they may tell you that the molestation took place "every time I was at Grandpa's house," or other such statements. To clarify that type of time frame/count statement, the parent of the child can tell you that they went to visit Grandpa every weekend, or every other weekend for the last six months, which will give you a time frame so that the District Attorney's Office can file criminal counts at a later time.

California law allows the prosecutor to file a general count of child molestation if it can be established that someone who is in a position to be a primary care provider for a child under the age of 14 years has molested that child three or more times over a period of time not less than three months. (Penal Code Sec. 288.5 - see your individual state laws.) However, it is still better from a criminal prosecution point of view if you can try to tie down an exact number of times that the molestation took place. (There will be further discussion of that issue in the next chapter.)

Time Frames

The rule of law is that you have to provide the suspect/defendant with an opportunity to say that he was out of town on the day that the alleged crime took place. Therefore, it is important to tie down, as accurately as possible, a general time as to when the crime took place. This may be as simple as the child saying; "it happened during Christmas vacation," or "it happened right after school started," or "it happened during the summer," or "it happened at the beach party," etc.

Secrets

Sometime during the course of the interview, you should ask the child if he or she was asked to keep the molestation secret. If so, you need to explain to the child the difference between a "good secret" and a "bad secret, and that it's okay to tell "bad secrets." You will also want to ask the child what they were told the consequences would be for telling the "bad secret," such as "you'll get into trouble," or, "grandpa will never be able to see you again," or, "the police department will come and take you away." Once aware of the threats, you can minimize the child's fear of telling by explaining what will *happen* and that grownups are responsible for what they do, not the kids. This eliminates the child's fear that they will be in trouble.

Other Victims

You should also ask the victim if he or she is aware of any other children that are being victimized. Sometimes, the children have actually witnessed siblings or other neighbor children being molested, and you want to try to identify those children.

Doing it Correctly

You'll know that you're doing it correctly when the kids start leaving their chair to sit in your lap. Usually, they want to draw something for you, so give them a new piece of paper and let them draw whatever they want. *Don't let them scribble on the evidence.* (The stick figure drawing will be booked into evidence later.)

Interview of Child 2-7 Years Using The Stick Figure System

You receive a radio call to "see the woman" with regard to a child molestation investigation. The radio call indicates that the reporting party, the child's mother, is stating that the child has been molested during a weekend visitation at the child's father's home; it also indicates that the suspect is the father's roommate.

When you arrive at the scene, you find that the mother is holding the five-year-old in her arms. You approach both mom and the child and you hold out your hand so that child can give you a "high five," while asking the child their age and telling them that they are "big for their age." You then speak very briefly with the mother to obtain the background information to confirm that it is the biological father's roommate who is the suspect and that the last molestation would have occurred a few days prior, during the last visitation.

Since the child will accept the world as it is presented to them, there is no need to carry on any extensive introductions between yourself and the child. Instead, simply tell the mother that you want to talk with the child at the dinner table, and enter the house to do just that. As described earlier, position yourself so that you and the child are sitting at the corners of the table.

Due to the age of the child, it is perfectly acceptable to have the mother present during this interview, but have her sitting across the table from you, as opposed to between you and the child. Never stand towering over the child, since this is an intimidating posture and the child is not likely to talk to you.

The next thing you do is trace hands with the child. First, trace the child's hand, then have the child trace your hand. In your police report, this hand tracing is referred to as "rapport building." The actual sketches of the hands do not need to be maintained as evidence.

You then ask the child to draw the stick figure with you, where you identify the body parts. Usually, I do the drawing, but if the child wants to actually draw in the hands, eyes, nose, let them do so. During this process, tell the child that if they don't know the answer to something, then it is okay for them to say, *"I don't know."* Giving them this option makes the interview "non-leading and non-suggestive."

Drawing with the child in this fashion helps build the interaction between you and the child. It also gives you an idea of how capable the child is in understanding concepts and what level of vocabulary you can use when talking with the child.

These initial interaction steps have nothing to do with the actual interview about the molestation itself. As a result, you have not infringed on the attention span of the child with reference as to how long the child will be able to talk to you about the actual molestation allegation.

Now, here's how the actual questioning about the molestation would transpire. After the stick figure has been completed, ask the child if it's "okay for someone to touch them on their hair." Hopefully, the child will say "yes." You might ask them if it's okay to touch them on the hands, and you can reach over and touch the child on the hand at the same time. And again you hope the child will say "yes." You then point to the genitals on the stick figure and ask the child if it's okay if someone touches them on their vagina. If the child says "no" you just continue on with other body parts to see if the child continues to state appropriate responses as to whether or not it's okay to be touched on the toes, feet, ankles, knees, etc.

Then go back to the genitals and ask if someone has ever touched them "there." If they answer "yes" then ask them who it was. The child should immediately respond with the first name of the suspect, e.g., Bill. Then ask the child a question that will identify the relationship of this child to the suspect, such as, "Where does this person live?" "Is this person a family member, like an uncle or cousin?"

That is normally about all the identifying information you will be able to get from a child this age.

Ask the child if this touching was part of a game they were playing, or if "Bill" was being "mean." If the child indicates that it was a game, you ask them what the name of the game was. Normally, they will say, "truth or dare," or "playing doctor." If "Bill was being mean," ask the child to explain this.

A third possibility is that the child was touched during bath time, or while the person was helping them get dressed, etc. If so, try to get the child to elaborate on that. Often, a parent assumes that any touching of their child's genitals was done as part of a molestation. However, the elements of a crime require that the child be touched "with the intent to sexually arouse either the child or the adult." If the touching took place as part of an attempt at hygiene or during the bathing process, you may not have a crime. The elements of a crime are usually met if the touching had no legitimate purpose.

You continue by asking the child if this has happened "a lot of times," or "a few times," and try to get the child to count for you or show you on her fingers how many times the molestation took place. You also have to ask the child if this touching took place over the clothing or "skin to skin." The way you do this is by asking the child, "Did you have your clothes on, or clothes off when it happened?" Also ask if the suspect had his clothes on or clothes off at the time this took place.

If dealing with a female victim, you now have to ask if there was any penetration of the vaginal area. Since the child will have no frame of reference as to what "inside" means versus "outside" of her body, this is a very difficult concept to get across to the child. I have found that the easiest way to do this is to use the index and middle finger on your left hand to represent the child's vagina, and then the index finger on your other hand to represent the suspect's hand or penis. You then take the right hand index finger and rub it on the outside of the other two fingers and ask the child, "Did he touch you on the *outside*?" while demonstrating, or, "Did he touch you on the *inside*?" while placing one index finger between the other two fingers. (Refer to Illustration # 9, page 37.) This has been the best way that I have found to get the child to understand the concept of what "inside her body" might mean.

You also have to ask the child what she was touched with. Don't assume that the touching was done with the hands or the genitals of the adult. Again, you do this by referring back to the stick figure, and ask, "Did Bill touch you with his fingers?" while pointing to the hands, or "Did he touch you with his nose, or with his tongue, or his mouth, or his penis, or his feet?"

By now, you will have used up the first four or eight minutes of your interview time with the child. The four to eight minute "clock" starts when the child states that their genitals were touched. As a result, you take them off subject by asking questions that will determine their qualification as a witness.

Point to their clothing and ask them, "Is that a blue shirt you're wearing?" " If I were to say that shirt is red, instead of blue, would that be the truth, or would that be a lie?" " Are you supposed to tell the truth or are you supposed to lie?" "What happens if you lie?" etc. This qualifying the child as a witness should take about a minute and suffices for taking the child's mind off of the molestation interview while, at the same time, not allowing them to become so engrossed in some other play activity where you cannot get them back on subject.

You can now determine if the suspect was naked. You do this by asking the child, "Did he have his clothes on, or his clothes off?" If the suspect was naked, you ask the child if she saw the suspect's penis. If the answer is yes, you have to ask if his penis was erect or non-erect. This is an important issue since it goes to show the sexual intent of the crime. Obviously, if the suspect is standing naked with an erection in front of a small child, it shows some sort of sexual intent on their part. Again, you have to demonstrate this with a child. You take your index finger and, in a hook shape, you show the child and ask the child, "Was his penis hanging down like this or was it sticking out straight?" (Refer to Illustration # 10, page 38.) Bend your finger down then stick it out straight, as a way of demonstrating the flaccid and the erect penis. Normally, the child will indicate that the penis was sticking out straight.

What I have also done on a number of occasions is ask the child to give me an idea as to the size of the suspect's penis by taking my two index fingers and indicating, "Is it real small, like this size?" (illustrating by putting your index fingers close together) or, "Is it real big?" (by putting your fingers, perhaps, several feet apart or somewhere in between). If the child is old enough to understand this concept, the child will generally put their two index fingers at a distance that will proximate the length of the suspect's penis. You then have the child put those two fingers down on the piece of paper that you have used to do the stick figure, and make a mark between the two fingers and later measure that distance to see how long the suspect's penis is. (Refer to Illustration # 8, page 36.) You might want to go so far as to have the child draw what the suspect's penis looks like. I have done this on several occasions and have gotten remarkably accurate representations of the suspect's penis. This is also a drawing that you should maintain as evidence.

Doing it this way will often generate some very interesting evidence items. I have had cases in which the children have drawn the suspect's penis to be very short and very curved, only to find out later that the suspect's genitals had been misshaped at birth and actually were deformed, as drawn by the child. The child might also draw some sort of tattooing or scarring, etc. around the genitals. This is one of the advantages to having the child interact with you by drawing the stick figure with you as opposed to using pre-drawns which may lead the child to an assumption that everybody's body looks the same.

Obviously, the older the child is, the more detail they will be able to give you about the suspect's genitals and the greater length of time you will have to interview the child on this subject.

At about this time, the child typically becomes fatigued again and you may be beginning to lose their attention. If you see this happening, take them off subject for a short time. This is an excellent opportunity to take a break and ask them about their family.

Specifically, ask them how many brothers and sisters they have, if the siblings are older or younger, what their names are, and if anyone else lives in their home, such as mother, father, aunt or uncle. This type of questioning should last for perhaps one to two minutes before you again bring the child back to the subject of the molestation. To allow them to do so for any longer would result in you "losing them."

Now, you will have a final opportunity to bring them back on subject for perhaps a minute or two to conduct some "cleanup" questions. These questions normally consist of a description as to where and when the molestation actually took place. Ask the child what room it took place in, such as the bedroom, kitchen or living room. Was it daytime or nighttime? Was it weekend or weekday? Was anyone else present? Did it happen on the bed, the floor, in the chair, etc.? (Young children respond best to short, closed questions and can easily give you one-or-two word responses.)

These are very important questions because if the child has been molested, they should be able to give you some of these associated details as to the environment surrounding the actual molestation. It could be as simple as the child stating that they were lying in bed when the suspect came in, pulled the covers off of them, and then fondled them. The child simply relating that the covers were removed from their body is an associated detail that helps establish that they were actually present when this happened and are relating factual details about what actually took place.

That is about all of the actual interview time you are going to have with the child. By now, the child is bored with the subject matter and only wants to play or draw, or talk about something other than the molestation allegation. You would now want to conduct some follow-up questions with the child's mother to further identify the suspect, find out how long that person has been a roommate of the biological father, how much she might know about him, where he works, what his phone number is, and similar types of identifying questions.

False Reports

With children of this age, sometimes you will get a false report. Generally it involves information given to the child by one parent who is in the middle of a heated custody dispute with the other parent. Children of this age really don't have the ability to lie. Lying implies an intent to deceive someone with some sort of purpose or reason to gain something by telling the lie. Children of this age really don't lie, even though they may say things that are not true. The easiest example of this is if a four-year-old tells you that Santa Claus came down the chimney last night and left Christmas presents under the tree. The child really is not lying to you, but at the same time, they are not saying something that they know to be true.

Sometimes, in a custody battle or divorce situation, one parent might actually coach the child to make up an allegation of molestation, or that parent will exaggerate what the child has stated about some touching that occurred during a weekend visitation. In this type of situation, the child will not be able to tell you the associated details of the molestation, such as: was the touching "good touching" or "bad touching?" Did it happen during the daytime or nighttime? Were the clothes on or the clothes off, etc.? That is why the interview process as described earlier is very important, since it does not imply the answers to any of the questions that you are asking the child.

It also allows you to discover if there has been a misinterpretation of the child's statement to the adult. The adult has interpreted the situation to indicate that there has been some sort of molestation when, in essence, there was no molestation. The touching was simply a part of some sort of hygiene problem, or did not happen at all.

After you have done several child molestation interviews, a "bad" case will stand out like a sore thumb. After a while, you will learn how a child normally relates a molestation incident to you and the type of details that a child should be able to give you about a molestation. When you find an interview that does not meet these normal standards that you are accustomed to seeing, you might suspect that there is a false report situation involved. You then need to ask the child's parent if there are any custody or other related problems between them.

A very important child development tip for interviewers is necessary as we discuss taking the report. When questioning a child and asking, "What happened next?" or, "Tell me everything that happened," you want to be cognizant that to many young children, time frames are irrelevant. "Next" to them may mean the incident that happened six months later; the unskilled interviewer may believe the child means the incident happened *immediately after* the one just reported. If you have not done so during the recounting of incidents, before you finish your interview, ask the child to help you narrow the time frames on each event. Tie down time frames by using a holiday or a family birthday to pinpoint the approximate date of the incident.

Repeating Questions

Children assume that adults know more than they do. For this reason, if you ask a child a question over and over again, the child will assume that they have given the wrong answer. They will assume this because had they given the right answer, an adult would *stop* asking the question. If you repeatedly ask a child the same question over and over again, they will change their answer. This does not mean they are lying to you; it is simply a part of the child abuse accommodation syndrome (a phrase coined after extensive research, teaching and writings by Dr. Roland Summit- see Ch. 7 and Bibliography). It is very common in young children. Defense attorneys are very aware of this and that is why they will ask a child the same question over and over again in an attempt to get them to change their answer. You, as an interviewer, have to be aware of this. Be sure that you don't ask the same question over and over again, because this will simply confuse the child and result in you getting conflicting responses.

Tape-recording / Videotaping

In my opinion, there is no need to tape-record or videotape any victim interview, either with a child or an adult. There is nothing in law that requires us to tape anything. Police officers do not routinely videotape burglary victims or robbery victims, and I don't see why we would need to tape-record child victims. I know that there are several different opinions in this regard, and that some agencies, especially some of the social service agencies, believe that videotaping is the right thing to do. Personally, I have found that this is more of a hindrance than a help.

The initial idea of videotaping or audio-taping the child victims was to eliminate the need for a child to be re-interviewed many times by different people throughout the protective services, protective custody and social services process. However, I have found that this is actually not the case. If you, as a the interviewer, *get all of the information, get it right, and get it the first time,* then that is sufficient as far as the details of the molestation that took place. By recording interviews, we have spoiled the defense attorneys. Since some agencies have routinely begun videotaping and audio-taping child molestation victims, there is an assumption that this is the standard practice and that there is some legal reason to do it. This is far from the truth.

The idea of videotaping and audio-taping child victims was sort of a knee-jerk response to poor interviews that were being conducted by law enforcement. It was thought that if you use some technical wizardry to record the interview with the child, this would somehow make that interview with the child better. In reality, if you tape-record a poor interview with a child, then you have made the situation worse, as opposed to better. If you follow the simple formula outlined earlier in your interview with the child, you should be able to *get all of the information* you need from the child, you *get it all correctly,* and you *get it all the first time.* Then there is really no need for a videotape or an audio-tape.

I have heard several people talk about success stories where playing the videotape forced the suspect to confess to a crime. I'm sure that's true, but I have many success stories where I have gotten suspects to confess to crimes where nothing was taped. I also know several horror stories in which the taping equipment failed and the interviewer forgot to take notes and has no clear recollection of the interview itself, because he thought the tape was going to capture the interview.

I have also seen many videotapes of policemen trying to interview children in child-friendly environments. One that stands out was an interviewer trying to talk to a teenage girl about having been molested for several years by her stepfather. The child-friendly environment that this police department had developed was two beanbag chairs sitting on the floor in an interview room that had a large clock mounted at floor level. This way, the camera, which was across the room, could actually monitor the time that the interview was taking place. However, the two people (the interviewer and the child) had to sit on opposite sides of the clock on these rather clumsy beanbag chairs. The tape of the interview clearly shows how the overweight and out of shape officer had trouble getting in and out of the beanbag chair, and how the girl spent most of the interview making sure that her legs were crossed so that the video would not show what was up her dress. Also, since they had to keep the clock between the two of them, there was no way for the two to interact at all, nor was there any way for the officer to take notes.

Trust me. Sit at the kitchen table, get all of the information, follow the method, (SFS) and you will be light years ahead of anyone who thinks that an interview can be improved upon by simply taping it.

Teaming with Social Services

Frequently, there will be a situation in which the social worker will want you to meet them at the home or school so they can conduct their interview at the same time you do. This is perfectly acceptable. There is no need to exclude the social worker from your interview. I have never experienced a problem where a social worker was called into court to be a witness where any sort of contradictory statements were made. The police officer has to remember, however, that he is in charge of the interview and he has the primary responsibility for obtaining the investigative information and for making a decision as to what type of crime report should be taken. The officer determines if the child should be taken into protective custody and if arrests should be made. The social worker should have some input into these decisions, but the ultimate decision and responsibility lies with the police officer. However, in cases with teamed interviews with social workers, a little bit of diplomacy goes a long way.

Protective Custody

Section 300 of the California Welfare and Institutions Code (see your individual state laws) details how a child should be taken into protective custody and under what circumstances. If you, as a police officer, make the determination that the child, for their protection, needs to be taken into protective custody, then you will have to do so per your department's protocols.

Normally, all you would have to do is fill out a simple petition form and then have the actual police report either attached to that form or have it faxed or forwarded to the foster home facility within a few hours of the child actually being delivered there.

The decision to take the child into protective custody is based on whether or not the child is going to be safe remaining at home. If the child is being molested by someone inside the home, and you arrest that person and remove them from the home, the child might be safe there. However, since the person might make bail or be released on their own recognizance, that is not a simple solution to the problem.

The problem with in-family molestation situations is that frequently the non-molesting parent is not going to take steps to adequately protect the child. It is not unusual for the wife in an incest situation to coerce the child into changing their story and to make every effort possible to bring the suspect back into the home once he has promised to "never do it again." You have to make an evaluation as to whether or not the parent is going to be protective of the child. The way you assess this is by trying to find out what type of action, if any, the parent took to protect the child once the disclosure of the molestation took place. If the mother protected the child by kicking her husband out and changing the locks on the doors and threatening to kill him if he returned, then you can assume that that mother is going to take steps to protect the child. If, however, the mother did absolutely nothing, told the child to keep it "our little secret," and then apologized to the suspect for walking in on him as he was having sex with the child, then you can assume that that parent is not going to

(1) Seating Arrangement for Interviewing Child

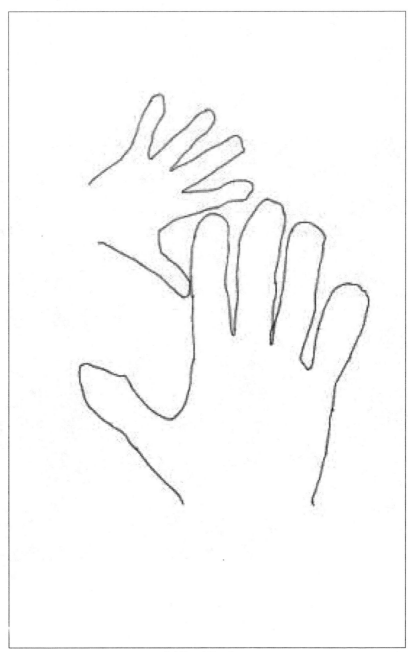

(2) Hand Tracings

(3) Stick Figure Identifying Body Parts

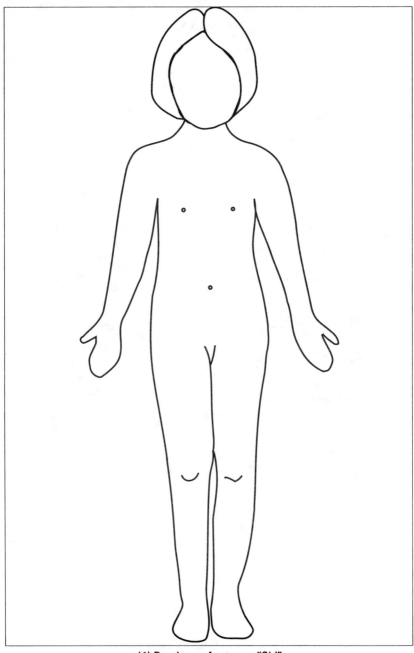

(4) Pre-drawn Anatomy, "Girl"

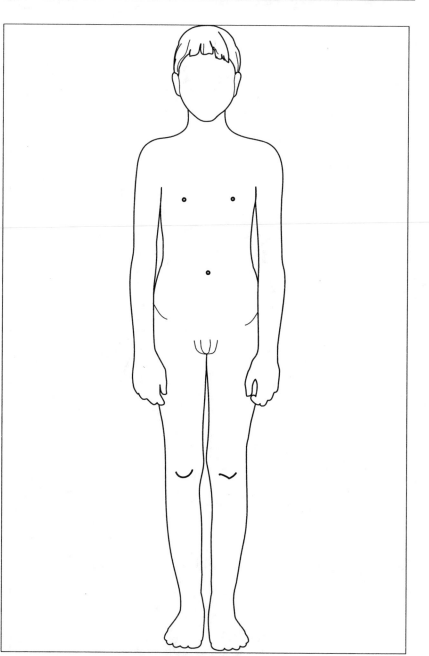

(5) Pre-drawn Anatomy, "Boy"

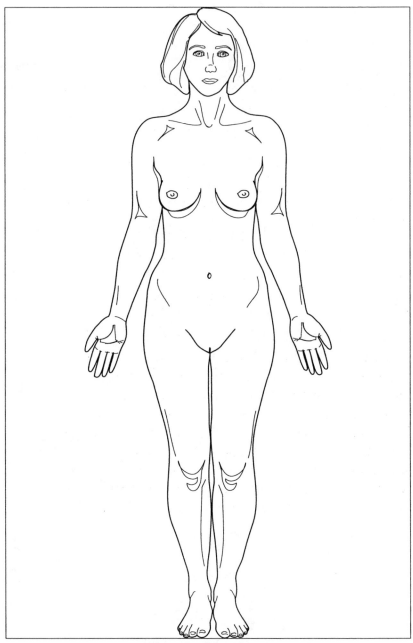

(6) Pre-drawn Anatomy, "Adult Female"

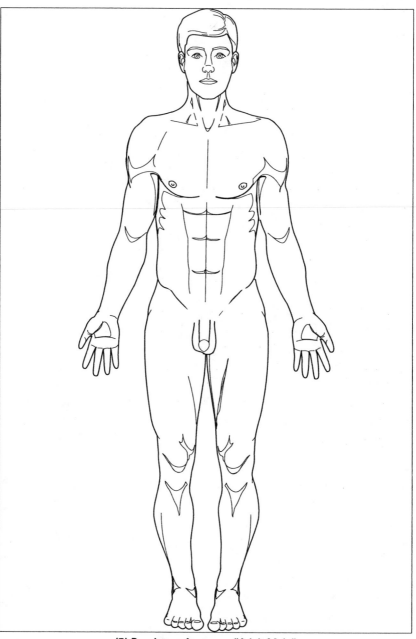

(7) Pre-drawn Anatomy, "Adult Male"

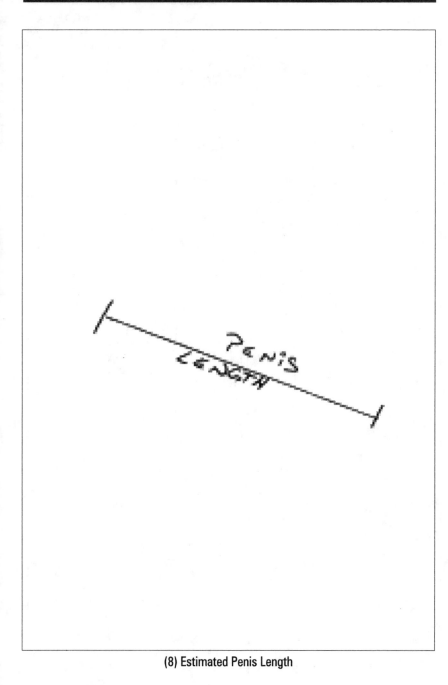

(8) Estimated Penis Length

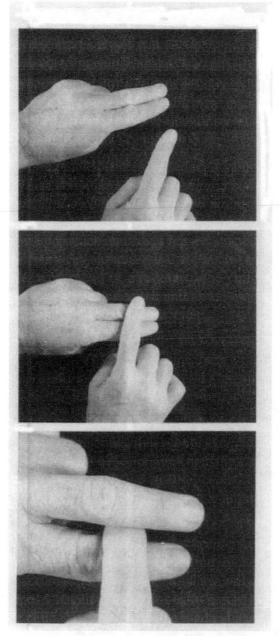

(9) Use of Fingers to Illustrate Vaginal Touching

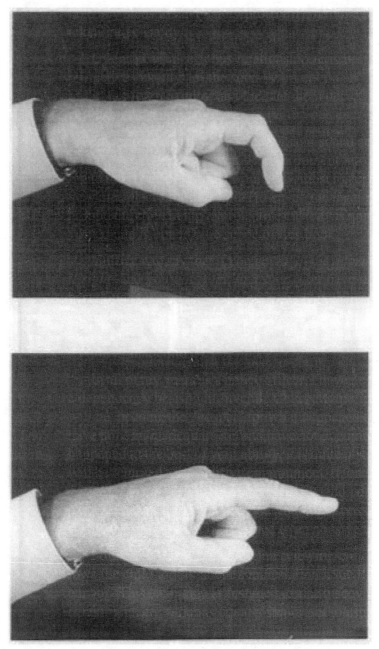

(10) Use of Fingers to Illustrate Flaccid and Erect Penis

take any steps to adequately protect the child, even if the suspect is taken into custody.

Often, in an incestuous relationship, it is best to put the child in protective custody, let the social workers do an in-depth evaluation of the family dynamics, and then let them decide whether or not the child should return home.

The protective custody situation and social services, in general, is a very complex, bureaucratic environment into which you are going to introduce the child. Fortunately, most foster home facilities are very nice places for the child. However, the legal fight that generates around the child being in protective custody is quite lengthy, very involved and is outside the scope of this book.

Suffice it to say that if you *got all of the information*, and *you got it right*, and you *got it the first time*, you have done absolutely the best thing you could ever do for the child who has been molested. To document what happened as thoroughly and accurately as possible is the best thing that you, as a police officer, can do for the further protection of that child.

In all of my years as a police officer, I have never had to testify at a dependency hearing in Juvenile Court. My police reports, as yours will be, become the "gospel" for what happened to that child. If you have done an inadequate job and have not documented what actually happened to the best of your ability, it is quite possible that that child will be returned to an abusive environment. If, on the other hand, you *got all of the information, got it all right,* and *you got it all the first time,* you have done the best that you could possibly do to see to it that that child will not be returned to an abusive environment.

Following this method for interviewing children of this age allows the child to talk about a molestation issue if, in fact, one is occurring. This technique is designed to also discover if no molestation is taking place, which is equally important to establish.

ASAV: Alleged Sexual Assault Victim Examination

"ASAV" is an acronym for Alleged Sexual Assault Victim examination. The procedure is used by hospital and nursing staff to determine the extent of sexual trauma to a victim's body when molestation or sexual assault has been alleged. The medical examination will discover any physical evidence as to vaginal or rectal injuries that will become corroborative evidence to your case.

When is it appropriate for a police officer to conduct a vaginal exam on a child? *NEVER! There is absolutely no reason for a police officer to examine the genitals of a child who has been molested.* This may sound like an over-simplification, but over the years, I have read many police reports in which an officer has conducted a vaginal exam on a three-or four-year-old to see if there is any evidence, or redness, soreness, tenderness, or swelling to the child's genitals that might be supportive evidence of the child's statement about being molested. *This is totally inappropriate.*

Not only does the medical community absolutely "flip out" when this happens, the police officer is doing exactly the same thing we are trying to send someone to prison for— touching a child's genitals when they have no business being down there.

An actual medical examination of a child's genitals, when done properly, will examine the internal structures of the child's genitalia. Redness to the outer labia/vagina is often meaningless in a molestation allegation. There are many reasons why the outer labia might be red, tender or swollen. Most of these reasons have absolutely nothing to do with being molested.

When the ASAV is conducted by qualified medical professionals, they look at the internal structures in an attempt to find thickening of the hymnal ring, any sort of tears, abrasions, etc. They will use a tool known as a colposcope to magnify the findings as a part of the internal examination of the child. They also have the medical background to render an opinion as to whether or not what they are seeing is evidence of a molestation or is normal for that child. Physicians have told me that hymens are like snowflakes…they are all unique and it takes an expert to distinguish one that has been damaged versus one that has not been. Also, because a lot of child molesting involves a simple fondling of the child with no actual penetration of the genitals or rectal area, it is not unusual for there to be no evidence, or no physical findings as a part of an ASAV examination. This negative finding, however, does not mean that a molestation did not occur.

There will be times when you go to speak to the parent of the molested child, and they will tell you that they (the parent) conducted a visual exam of the child's genitals and they saw some redness, swelling, or tenderness. You can note that in your police report as being a factual thing that they saw, but don't conclude for a minute that seeing some redness to the outer labia is any proof whatsoever that there was a molestation.

In a situation where a child has been forcibly raped and is bleeding or needs immediate medical attention, take that child to the emergency room for medical treatment. If emergency room treatment is not necessary, then follow the normal protocols for handling any rape victim. Normally, this involves taking the child to a location where a rape examination can be done so that biological samples can be obtained for evidence purposes.

In Orange County, California, the CAST (Child Abuse Services Team) services are available on a twenty-four-hour-a-day basis. The office itself is only open during normal business hours, but there is a round-the-clock call-out procedure that can be followed. If the CAST facility is not available, Martin Luther Hospital has trained medical personnel on staff around the clock who can conduct a forensic exam of a child's genitals to collect biological evidence left by the suspect (seminal fluid) and can photograph and document any genital tearing or injuries. Most counties have similar services available to them. It's important for the investigator to be familiar with the capabilities of the various medical facilities in their local area.

An immediate exam is not needed if the molestation has been ongoing and the last incident occurred three or more days ago. In this situation, it's best to document your interview and let the assigned investigator make the decision about having a medical exam done.

Interviews at School

If you are called to a school to interview a child because of an allegation of molestation, it is in most cases perfectly legal to interview that child at school without the parents' permission, consent or knowledge. Obviously, if the molester is someone within the child's home, you will need to talk to that child outside of the home, so the school is the logical place to do that.

Some states are considering legislation that would require school officials to advise parents of an on-campus police interview. The exception normally built into these laws is that <u>NO</u> notification is to be made if the suspect is a family member.

There are occasions when there has been a disclosure of a molestation late in the afternoon and the child is sent home prior to Social Services and/or the police arriving at school. If the information is that the child is being molested at home, often it is better to wait until the next day when the child is back at school to interview them. Although this does set up a situation where the child could be victimized again prior to your interview, the odds of you obtaining the information that you need to protect the child for the long term is better if you wait until the following day.

If the molestation interview is conducted at school, follow the same formula/protocol as indicated earlier in this chapter.

Cross-reporting to the Child Abuse Registry

California State law requires that you, as a mandated reporter of child abuse, contact the Child Abuse Registry by phone as soon as possible once you have learned of a child being sexually molested, physically abused, emotionally abused, or neglected. As soon as you have an opportunity to get to a telephone, you should call the Child Abuse Registry and supply them with the basic information they ask you over the phone. The person answering the phone will obtain the child's name, address, date of birth, the parents' information, and a brief synopsis as to what occurred. The social worker will also want to know if there is a need for an immediate response by the Social Services to come to meet you or if the child is going to be taken into protective custody.

California Penal Code Sec. 11166(i) requires that within thirty-six hours of this telephone report, the police reports and the appropriate forms for Social Services be mailed to the Child Abuse Registry (see your individual state laws for reporting requirements). Normally, this forwarding of the police reports is left to Detective personnel and/or Records personnel. Orange County Child Abuse Registry will accept a faxed copy in lieu of a mailed copy, but I encourage you to keep a copy of your transmission report. Additionally, some jurisdictions have made it a practice to document the name of the person at Social Services that took the telephone report. That's not a bad idea! Various states and counties have similar protective networks in place.

Photographs as Evidence

During the course of your interview with the child, you should ask the child if any photographs were taken of him/her during the course of the molestation. You would also want to ask the child if any photographs of nude children or nude adults engaged in sexual acts were shown to them by the suspect prior to or during the course of that child's victimization. Obviously, this would be important information to know so that these photos can be seized, usually during the service of a search warrant.

Report Narrative: 2-7 Year Old Victim

On 09-15-97 at 1500 hours, I met with victim 97-123 (Sarah) and her mother at home regarding a radio call report that Sarah was being molested during her weekend visitations at her father's home in Orange County. Sarah's mother told me that the suspect in this case was Sarah's biological father's roommate, Bill Smith. Sara's mother also provided identifying information on the suspect.

I interviewed Sarah while seated at the dining table inside the family home. After establishing rapport with her, I asked her if she could help me draw a stick figure of a girl. With Sarah's help, I completed a stick figure drawing, during which time we identified body parts, including her vaginal area, which she refers to as her "butterfly." Sara was also able to distinguish between "bad" and "good" touching.

I asked Sarah if anyone had ever touched her vaginal area in a "bad way." Sarah told me that someone had. She identified this person as being "Bill," adding that "Bill" is someone who lives with her father. She told me that every time she goes to visit with her father, "Bill" touches her on her vaginal area.

Sarah continued to state that this touching consisted of "Bill" using his hand to touch her on her vagina. She indicated that this happened in a skin-to-skin fashion, since he would remove her clothing just prior to touching her. I then used my index and middle fingers on my left hand to represent Sarah's vagina, and the index finger on my right hand to represent the suspect's finger. Rubbing the index finger of my right hand on the other two fingers, I asked Sarah if the touching occurred on the outside of her vagina, or if it occurred with the suspect putting his fingers inside her vagina. Sarah stated that the suspect put his fingers inside her vagina and indicated that he only put it in "a little bit." She did this by showing me, with her index finger, that he only penetrated the vagina perhaps one-half inch, or so, with his finger.

I asked Sarah if "Bill" had his clothes on or off at the time he was touching her. She told me that he would pull his "wiener" out of his pants as he was touching her. I used the same stick figure to identify his "wiener" as being his penis. Sarah went on to state that his penis was "sticking out straight" at the time that she saw it.

I asked Sarah if she touched "Bill's" penis during this time. She said that she did. I then used my ball point pen to represent the suspect's penis and asked Sarah to show me how she touched it. Sarah told me that the suspect took her hand and placed it on his penis, and while his hand was on top of hers, he moved her hand in an up-and-down motion on his penis. She demonstrated this to me using the ball point pen. I asked Sarah if anything came out of the suspect's penis while doing this, and she stated that the "white sticky stuff" came out.

I then asked Sarah if she could give me an approximation as to how big the suspect's penis was. I did this by using my two index fingers to represent a general length. Sarah, using her index fingers, showed me her representation of how long the suspect's penis was. I then had her place both of her index fingers down onto a piece of paper and I drew a line between the two index fingers. I later measured this distance and found it to be 6" long.

I asked Sarah if she could draw the suspect's penis for me, and she said she could. On the back of the piece of paper that the stick figure was drawn on, she drew me her representation of the suspect's penis. She identified his "wiener" and also drew what she referred to as "balls."

Sarah went on to state that the molesting took place in the suspect's bedroom. She told me that the suspect would take her in the bedroom, assist her in taking off her clothes, and then he would touch her in a skin-to-skin fashion with his hand. Sarah said that her father was out of the home when this took place, and she believed he was at the store or at work at the time the sexual touching took place.

Sarah went on to tell me that the touching took place on top of the suspect's bed and that he had a red blanket or bedspread on it. She added that the suspect told her this was a "secret game" that they were playing and that she should not tell anyone about it. The suspect also told her that if she told anyone about the game, that she (Sarah) might get into trouble.

I asked Sarah how many times this type of touching took place. She held up five fingers, saying it happened "that many times." At this point, Sarah's mother, who was present during the interview, indicated that she has been separated from her husband for the past six months, and that Sarah goes and visits him every weekend. She stated that about three months ago, the suspect, "Bill," became a full-time roommate at the father's home.

During the course of the interview, I also questioned Sarah as to whether or not she knew the difference between the truth and a lie. I noted that she was wearing a blue shirt. I pointed to her shirt and asked her what color it was. She correctly answered by saying it was blue. I asked her that if I were to say that the shirt was red instead of blue, would that be the truth or would it be a lie? She told me that that would be a lie. I then asked her if she was supposed to tell the truth or supposed to lie. She said that you are always supposed to tell the truth. I asked her what happens if she does not tell the truth, and she said that Mommy puts her in time-out if she lies.

Sarah said that no pictures were taken of her, nor was she shown pictures of other people. She also told me that the suspect only touched her vaginal area with his hand, as opposed to any other part of his body.

Due to the nature of the molestation as described by Sarah, I did not make arrangements for a medical examination to be conducted at this time. I did call the Child Abuse Registry and spoke with the on-duty worker, James Bullwinkle, and made a telephone report of the molestation incident to him. Sarah was not taken into protective custody at this time. I advised her mother not to allow any further visitations at the father's home until the police investigation could be completed.

CHAPTER 3

INTERVIEWING CHILDREN AGES 8 - 12

Eight-to twelve-year-olds are obviously more verbal than the younger children, so there is no need to go through as extensive a rapport establishing process. However, it is important to develop a friendly non-threatening relationship before beginning the interview.

Background

As before, obtain what background information you can from the reporting party with regard to the molestation allegation.

Seating Arrangement

The seating arrangement with the child should be the same, although you might not want to sit quite as close to them and you don't want them crawling in your lap toward the end of the interview. Also, there is no need to trace hands or to draw a stick figure with a child of this age to identify body parts. However, it is necessary to identify some general terms with them.

Terminology

Since, as we have discussed, an officer may testify at the preliminary hearing for the child, you will have to establish that you did clarify the terms used in your report with the child. A child merely telling you that they had "sex" with the suspect is not sufficient. You will have to identify that "sex" means "sexual intercourse," and that this term means the suspect placed his penis into the vagina of the child. You will also have to establish a definition for "oral copulation," "sodomy," or any other terms you've used in your report that the child might have disclosed to you in their language.

Teaming with Social Services

If the child is disclosing an in-family molestation situation, it is quite likely that this information will come forward at school. You might want to consider "teaming" with Social Services so that the protective custody issues can be dealt with at the same time that the criminal investigation/interview is done.

Out-of-Home Suspect

It is quite possible that the child is going to disclose an ongoing molestation situation with multiple sexual acts over an extended period of time. This is because a child of this age is out of the view of the parents for a greater length of time, either going to school or going to Little League practice, Scouts, or other activities away from home. These children are also being watched in after-school day care situations. It is also possible that the child has been targeted by a stepparent who has entered the family with the specific purpose of having sex with the child. You should be prepared to conduct a rather lengthy interview with this child, because they will be disclosing to you multiple acts which occurred over an extended length of time.

Victim / Suspect Profile

Long-term molestation situations may go undetected for a long time. This is often due to the profile of the victim and the manipulative nature of the predator. Statistically, a child victim of long-term molestation criminal activity will be one who is feeling neglected at home and not having his or her emotional needs or concerns met. As a result, the child tends to seek out someone who *will* pay attention. Unfortunately, many times they will find a child molester to give them the emotional pat on the back they seek. In exchange for that positive input from the adult, the child has to allow the sexual touching.

As stated before, there are several types of sexual offenders and we encourage you to read several of the books listed in the bibliography that discuss, in detail, the profile of sexual predators. Nicholas Groth (*Sexual Assault of Adolescents and Children*) states in his book, and we strongly agree with him, that in order to understand the crime, you must understand the criminal. Suffice it to say, for this textbook purpose, sexual predators come in all shapes and sizes, may be either sex, exist in all ethnic and educational levels and can be found as often in a church as in a farm environment. They may be boy scout leaders, priests, construction workers, ministers, teachers or police officers. Only two of the most common offenders will be discussed in any detail in the subsequent text for purposes of better investigation reports and to provide the investigator enough information to adequately ask the right questions.

The common factor with all offenders is that they *seek out vulnerable children from whom they receive their emotional and sexual gratification.*

Victim Gender

My experience has been that there are an equal number of male and female victims. This means that a suspect may molest both males and females, or he may exclusively molest one or the other sex. If you are dealing with an in-family molestation situation where one of the girls has come forward to talk about a molestation allegation, you obviously have to talk to all of the girls in the home. You also have to talk to the boys. Sex offenders have a tendency to see children as a non-sexual group unto themselves. This means that they do not see the children as being boy children and girl children; they simply see them as one group, as "children." For this reason, they are equally vulnerable, and both sexes have to be interviewed once there has been a disclosure of a molestation within a family.

Family Dynamics

Since victims are more verbal at this age, they should be able to give you a lot of detail about the dynamics of the family situation and of the relationship between themselves and the suspect. This is very important information for the person who is going to interview the suspect later on.

Number of Counts

A child of this age will be able to detail with some accuracy the number of times there has been sexual contact between the child and the adult. Generally, you first ask the child when the last time any sexual contact took place. This will normally be a few days, or perhaps a week or two prior to your interview. Then you would ask the child when their very first time was. The child is normally able to recall a general time frame as to when the very first sexual act took place. You then try to tie down other time frames by asking, "Do you recall a time when there was a molestation during Christmas vacation or perhaps Easter, the end of the school year, during the summer, between the 4th and 5th grades, or right at the time school started, at Halloween, or Thanksgiving?"

It is not sufficient just to say that there were "about a hundred sexual contacts between the suspect and the child." What you should try to do is tie down each incident that the child can remember, within a time frame, as a specific crime detailing what actually took place at that time. This allows the District Attorney to file multiple counts against the suspect during those time frames.

Attention Span

With a child of this age, there is not as much need to be as concerned about them becoming fatigued or being unable to pay attention to the interviewer over an extended length of time. However, if the interview is going to be very lengthy, you might want to take a break for a few minutes and get up and walk around with the child, or talk about something else for a couple of minutes just to give you and the child a little time to relax from the tension of the interview.

Qualifying as a Witness

A child of this age normally does not need to be qualified as a witness. It is assumed that someone this age already knows the difference between telling the truth and telling a lie. However, if the child has some sort of disability or handicap or mental problem that you think might allow the issue to be raised in court, then you should go ahead and qualify the child as a witness as you would do with a much younger child.

Fixated Pedophile

A fixated pedophile is a person who has, from adolescence, been sexually attracted primarily or exclusively to significantly younger people and this attraction has persisted throughout his life regardless of what other sexual experiences he has had.

If the child has been involved with a fixated pedophile, most likely the child has been involved in a long-term sexual relationship with this person. There has probably been a lengthy seduction-type process and then a peer-type relationship. You should inquire of the child as to what type of non-sexual activities that he and the adult did together. In this type of relationship, it would not be unusual for the suspect to let the child drive his car. They might sneak into the movies together or play video games together, with the adult acting at a social level to the age of the child. This is additional information that should be incorporated in your report, in addition to the actual recalling of the sexual contacts.

Regressed Pedophile

A regressed pedophile is a person who originally preferred peers or adult partners for sexual gratification; however, when conflict enters into these adult relationships, the adult sexual partners are replaced by a child for the focus of their sexual interest and desire. (Definitions taken from "Sexual Assaults of Children and Adolescents" by Burgess, Groth, Holdstrom and Sgroi. See Bibliography.)

This type of offender is someone who will normally assault children of the opposite sex. The sexual contact may have occurred only a few times, or he may regressed several times over a period of years.

Other Types of Molesters

There are many other types of people who molest children. Some of them are rapists who actually, in a clinical definition, rape children within their own family. It is not unusual to find someone who would be clinically diagnosed as a "rapist," who is having ongoing sexual contact with his own children. One might first think that this person is a "pedophile." when, in reality, he is actually a rapist. There are also numerous other types of categories of people who have sexual contact with children, so be sure not to discount statements given to you by the child as to the dynamics of the relationship between them and the offender.

Discussion

When you receive a call that is going to put you in contact with a child of this age range, you will have to assume that you are going to be involved in a rather lengthy interview process. Assume at least a forty-five minute interview with the child.

Even if the child is being molested by someone outside of his family, such as a neighbor, coach or scout leader, you may have to take the child into protective custody, depending on the parents' ability to protect the child and keep him away from the offender. Often, these children are "throw away" children. The parents may not be terribly protective of the child once the molestation has been disclosed. It is this lack of concern on the part of the parent that has led to the molestation.

Although you will not have to identify body parts in the same fashion as you do with younger children, you should not overlook the possibility that the older child can give you more description as to what the suspect's body actually looks like. If there are scars, tattoos, birthmarks, or deformities that the child has witnessed, you should solicit this information from the child, since it is very important corroborative evidence to the molestation allegation. You should also question the child as to whether or not he or she has been photographed by the suspect, when the last time they saw these photographs, and where the photographs are kept. This will allow a search warrant to be prepared to look for those evidentiary items.

Cross-Reporting

This type of molestation situation has to be cross-reported to the Child Abuse Registry, just like any other allegation of child abuse. If the child is being victimized by someone inside their family, Social

Services will normally respond within two hours to help make a determination as to whether or not the child should be taken into protective custody. If the child is being victimized by an out-of-family perpetrator, frequently, they will respond within ten days, as opposed to immediately.

Number of Counts

It is not unusual for a child in this age range to only tell you about 25% of the actual times there was sexual contact between them and the adult. There is a tendency to downplay the severity of the molestation, either by reducing the number of times there was sexual contact, or minimizing the sexual contact to fondling, when there was actual intercourse or oral sex. It is important that you tell the child that you need to know all of what took place so that you can get a complete picture of what was actually transpiring. If you fail to *get it all*, you may be faced with additional allegations surfacing during court testimony.

When the child testifies in court to a different set of molestation incidents than they told you about, a problem exists. The child is not lying; he is simply telling the other 75% of what actually took place. As a result, *if you did not get it all, get it right* and *get it all the first time,* it makes the child look as if he were lying in court. It is important to explain this to the child so they will feel more comfortable in telling you as much as they can actually recall during that initial interview.

When you write the police report, make an allowance for the other 75% of the story. You do this by giving a general overview of the molestation in the first part of your report. An example of this would be, "The victim said that he had sex with the suspect three times a week for the last six months." If the victim can only detail one or two of these actual molestations during that time frame, you then become more specific about those incidents that they can specifically recall. This way, in court, when the victim recalls more specific incidents than he did during your interview, it doesn't make it look like they are lying.

False Reports

False reports by children in this age range are relatively rare, in my experience. This is because they are not so easily influenced by adults as younger children are. Since they already know that Santa Claus does not leave presents under the tree, they are not as likely to be influenced by a parent during a custody dispute to believe that they were molested when, in fact, they were not. However, if you do see a false report in this area, it generally revolves around a custody-type of situation.

Interview: 8-12 Year-Old Victim

The officer receives a call to meet with a social worker at a grammar school regarding the possible molestation of a nine-year-old boy. Upon arrival, the officer should meet with the social worker and obtain a general overview of the allegations. In this way, the interview will not be contaminated. You should tell the school officials to *NOT CALL THE PARENTS* because of the possibility that they might be suspects and/or the officer may have to take the child into protective custody. You don't want to find yourself in a situation where an angry parent bursts into the middle of your interview telling the kid to "*Shut Up*" before you have established the elements of a crime.

Find a private room in which to conduct the interview. I prefer to use a conference room because it generally has a larger table. This enables me to use the preferred table corner seating arrangement, allowing me to sit at 90° to the child. By using the conference or meeting room rather than an office, there is less chance you will be interrupted by a phone ringing or someone's need to "interrupt for just a moment" to obtain papers from their desk.

At first you don't sit too close to the child and ask a few introductory questions about his family, school and outside activities in order to establish rapport and get an idea of his or her language level and maturity. Tell the child that the social worker has told you about the molestation allegations but that you need more information so that the child can help you figure out what happened and what to do next. When you start to ask about the molestation, move closer to the child and let him see that you are taking notes which indicates you are interested in what he has to say. The written notes, however, should be very brief so that the silence while you write does not cause long pauses in the conversation.

I usually start by asking the child how he first met the suspect, and when the sexual touching first started. I then tell the child, "I need to be sure that I understand you." which leads you into a conversation to define terms for genitals and the sexual acts. I then get a general overview of the allegations and tie down more specifics/time frames. I always close the conversation by asking the child if they have any questions of me.

Report Narrative: 8 - 12 Year Old Victim

On 8-23-96, at 1130 hours, I went to Sunnyvale School and met with Social Worker Randy Snodgrass. Snodgrass told me that he had been called to the school by the school nurse regarding the disclosure of an ongoing sexual molestation of a nine-year-old boy, Victim #96-102 (Ryan).

Ryan had disclosed to the school nurse that after school each day, he was being baby-sat by a neighbor who had routinely been having sexual contact with him. Apparently, Ryan had disclosed the molestation to his family several weeks ago and they responded by telling Ryan to simply "stay away from him," but continued to allow him to go over to the suspect's residence. I then had Ryan brought into the room, where Social Worker Snodgrass and I spoke to him. I found Ryan to be a bright and articulate nine-year old whose mannerisms were age appropriate.

By way of background information, Ryan told me that approximately a year ago, his mother started to work a full-time job during the day. Arrangements were made for him to go to a neighbor's house after school. The neighbor had volunteered free after-school day care for Ryan between about 3:00 p.m. and 6:00 p.m. Ryan identified the suspect, as indicated on the face page, as a male, white, in his mid 30's.

Ryan went on to state that initially, his contacts with the suspect consisted of the suspect helping Ryan with his homework and playing video games. As time went on, the suspect began to have Ryan sit on his lap as they played video games. The suspect began to rub the inside of Ryan's thighs over his clothing and ultimately began touching Ryan's genitals over his clothing. Ryan stated that he had been at the suspect's residence for approximately one month before the actual touching of his genitals took place.

Ryan told me that as the sexual touching progressed, both he and the suspect would take their clothes off in both the living room and sometimes in the bedroom of the suspect's home. They would then engage in mutual oral sex and masturbation of each other. Ryan indicated that initially, the suspect stated he wanted to teach Ryan "how to masturbate." The suspect would disrobe in front of Ryan and masturbate his own penis until he ejaculated. The suspect would then undress Ryan and then masturbate him in a similar fashion. As the relationship continued, the suspect convinced Ryan that he (Ryan) should masturbate the suspect's penis while, at the same time, the suspect masturbated Ryan.

Ryan continued, that about two months ago, the sexual relationship escalated to where the suspect began performing oral sex on Ryan. Ryan stated that there were approximately ten times where the suspect performed oral sex on Ryan's penis. Ryan went on to state that about two weeks ago, the suspect asked Ryan to perform oral sex on him. Ryan did, in fact, put his mouth on the suspect's penis on three different occasions within the last two weeks.

Ryan stated that the last time there was any sexual activity between him and the suspect was last Friday. He said that during that particular incident, he went to the suspect's house after school and the suspect invited him into the his bedroom. At that time, both Ryan and the suspect disrobed and the suspect orally copulated Ryan's penis for perhaps ten minutes. The suspect then sat down on the bed, removed his own pants, and asked Ryan to orally copulate him. Ryan orally copulated the suspect's penis for two or three minutes and then masturbated the suspect until he ejaculated.

Ryan estimated that the first time there was any actual sexual contact between him and the suspect would have been about a month and a half to two months after the start of the school year of 1995. He stated that the sexual acts then continued three or four times a week, every week, for the next year or so.

Ryan specifically recalls that on the Friday after Thanksgiving of 1995, he was going to spend the entire day at the suspect's residence, since both of his parents were going to be out of town. On this particular day, Ryan stated that while playing video games in the suspect's living room, the suspect masturbated Ryan twice and had Ryan masturbate the suspect on two separate occasions.

Ryan also stated that during Christmas break of 1995, there were numerous times when he had sexual contact with the suspect. Ryan specifically recalls one incident that occurred in the evening hours at the suspect's residence. He stated that he had had dinner at the suspect's house that night and, after dinner, the suspect took him into the bedroom. At this time, the suspect removed Ryan's pants, orally copulated him while inserting one finger into Ryan's rectum. After the suspect orally copulated Ryan for about five minutes, Ryan masturbated the suspect until he ejaculated.

Ryan went on to state that on his birthday, in March of 1996, the suspect took him out to a movie. On the way home from the movie, the suspect parked his vehicle in a closed commercial area, approximately one-half mile away from Ryan's home. While in this darkened commercial area, the suspect orally copulated Ryan's penis and Ryan then masturbated the suspect until he ejaculated.

Ryan indicated that his sexual contacts with the suspect continued on a weekly basis throughout the remainder of the school year and throughout the first month or so of the summer of 1996. Ryan stated that he became increasingly uncomfortable with the sexual contact by the suspect and that the suspect wanted more oral sex from Ryan.

Ryan stated that he finally told his parents about the sexual victimization. He stated that his parents did not seem overly concerned about this and simply told him to refuse any further sexual contacts with the suspect. They told him to continue going to the suspect's house for after-school day care purposes, but to simply refuse any further sexual contact with him. Ryan stated that he attempted to refuse the sexual advances by the suspect after that time; however, they continued and became more severe since Ryan now began performing oral sex on the suspect.

Ryan also indicated that several times during his relationship with the suspect, the suspect showed him commercially produced photographs of nude adults in magazines. These adults were engaged in both vaginal and anal intercourse, along with oral sex. The pictures included both heterosexual and homosexual activity. Ryan added that about six months ago, the suspect did convince him to pose nude for some Polaroid-type photographs. Ryan stated that these photographs are kept in a shoe box underneath the suspect's bed in his residence. The last time Ryan saw these photographs was about three months ago.

Nothing further was gained from the interview with Ryan. It was decided by the social worker and me that he should be taken into protective custody since it did not appear that his parents were willing to protect him from the suspect. Ryan does not have any siblings and he was unaware of any other children who were being molested by the suspect at this time.

CHAPTER 4

INTERVIEWING AGES 13 - 18

Background Information

This generally tends to be more sketchy than with the younger children due to reluctance on the part of the victim to openly disclose details of the molestation to anybody. The victims tend to understand the sexual and social nature of the offense and society's general phobia about sexual acts in general. As a result, they are a little more reluctant to be open about what has taken place.

If the child has been involved in a long-term sexual relationship with the suspect, there is a great possibility that they will have some *positive* feelings about the offender. They will also have some guilt feelings about divulging the relationship and their participation in it. These long-term relationships involve a coercion into the sexual activity by a non-complaining victim, as opposed to the forced sexual victimization in a one-time rape-type scenario.

For this reason, you again run into a situation in which the child is normally willing to talk about 25-30% of the actual numbers of sexual acts. As previously stated, this creates a problem in court when, as the child is more comfortable later in revealing more of what took place, they talk about added sexual encounters that they did not give the initial officer.

First Contact with the Victim

These children are old enough to understand why you are there and that you have been called to the scene to interview them with regards to the molestation situation. Introducing yourself by name and explaining the purpose of your visit is normally all of the introduction you need with children in this age range. Children of this age span are often fearful, suspicious or even have a dislike of law enforcement, so some friendly discussion of a general nature may help to establish a degree of rapport which will enable you to begin the interview.

Building Rapport with a Teen

The simplest way to develop rapport with a teenage molestation victim is to treat them "like a real person." This may sound like an oversimplification, but if you approach them in a business-like manner and talk to them like young adults, you will accomplish your goal of gathering as much information as possible.

These teens have been treated like sex "objects" for a large part of their lives. They've been lied to, manipulated, used and thrown away. What they don't want is for some officer to be condescending, aloof, arrogant, indignant or judgmental. Don't pat them on the head and tell them to be a "nice little girl" or tell them "tell me what happened and I'll make it better." Talking down to them like that is a form of manipulation that they'll see right through and probably decide not to talk to you.

Also, do not try to win them over by telling them how angry or disgusted you are with someone who would "do something like that" to a child. That type of statement is a double-edged sword that cuts two ways, both bad. First, the victim may have some positive feelings for the suspect. If so, you've just thrown up another hurdle between you and the child. Secondly, those "disgusting acts" are something that she or he has been doing for a long time. As a result, the child will assume that you are angry and disgusted at them too and see them as something less than human.

The point is that the teenage molestation victim will not be able to make the subtle distinction between your disgust for the suspect and your feelings toward them.

Manipulation by Victims

Some of the victims who have been involved in long-term relationships, especially in an in-family type situation, have learned to be very manipulative of adults and of their environment. If that has been the case with the child you are dealing with, they will also attempt to manipulate you during the course of the interview.

With that in mind, you have to put on your "no nonsense face." This means that you have to take charge of the situation without being overbearing. You have to let the child know that you have a legitimate reason for knowing the intimate details of what took place and that you are not going to accept anything less than that.

These children have learned that they can frequently avoid any scrutiny by adults by simply smiling or giving a passive type of answer without any great detail. Let the child know by your demeanor that you are not going to allow that to happen. You also have to let them know that you have heard "everything" before and you are not going to be embarrassed by what the child has to say, nor are you going to be critical of their involvement in an ongoing sexual relationship.

You can also tell the child that since you are familiar with all of the "street language" that they might know, it is okay for them to use that type of terminology. However, once again, you might want to identify terms just to be absolutely certain that you are talking about the same things. Once you have identified their common terms for actual sexual acts, you should use the more clinical terms for the remainder of your report. Also, if you begin to use the clinical terms during the course of your interview (e.g., intercourse versus "screw"), the victim has a tendency to begin using those terms also. This helps the victim distance themselves from the actual emotional impact of the events and it prepares them for courtroom testimony.

Sample Narrative: Manipulative Teenage Victim

On 10-16-97, at 0930 hours, I met with victim 97-125, Jennifer, a fourteen-year-old female, and her mother, Mrs. Carlson, at their home. Mrs. Carlson stated that she was concerned that her daughter was sexually active with Mrs. Carlson's second husband (Jennifer's stepfather, identified as the suspect).

Mrs. Carlson stated she became suspicious last week when she received a telephone call from Jennifer's school. Apparently, Jennifer had not been attending class for the last several weeks. Mrs. Carlson was totally unaware of this. She stated that it was a normal routine for the suspect to take Jennifer to school on his way to work.

When Mrs. Carlson learned that the suspect had been calling the school and indicating that Jennifer was sick each day, she felt something was going on.

Mrs. Carlson went on to explain that over the last several months, she has become concerned about the closeness of the relationship between Jennifer and the suspect. She stated it is not unusual for them to hold hands when they are out in public together and he seems to be addressing her more like a girlfriend rather than a stepdaughter.

I questioned Mrs. Carlson about her relationship with the suspect. She told me that they have been married for the last four years. She married him shortly after her divorce from a very abusive first husband, Jennifer's biological father. Since the divorce, she has not had any contact with Jennifer's biological father, nor has he had any contact with Jennifer. Mrs. Carlson stated that when she married the suspect, it was more a marriage of convenience rather than of love. She stated that her sexual activity with the suspect is very infrequent. She stated she married him more because he was very nice to Jennifer and he made very few demands of her, either sexually or otherwise. Mrs. Carlson saw this as a welcome relief from the relationship she had with her abusive first husband.

Mrs. Carlson went on to say that in the last six to eight months, it had not been unusual for the suspect to come to the breakfast table wearing female clothing. She stated that he would often explain that it was because she was "frigid" and that he needed to wear this apparel to relieve his sexual needs. She also saw him masturbating frequently while wearing women's clothing.

Mrs. Carlson stated that when she realized that Jennifer was not going to school, she feared that perhaps there was more going on between the suspect and Jennifer. With that in mind, she began to search through the suspect's belongings and in his closet. She found a locked briefcase which she forced open and found approximately one hundred (100) photographs inside. Many of the photographs were of Jennifer posing nude, and some were of Jennifer involved in sexual activity with the suspect.

Mrs. Carlson stated that last night, she had confronted her husband with the photographs. He became very angry at her, telling her that she had no business prying into his personal property. The suspect then collected many of his personal belongings, including the briefcase with the photos inside, and moved out of the home. Mrs. Carlson stated that she had kept a half dozen of the photographs and had them in her purse. She gave them to me for evidence purposes. I saw that these photographs were sexually explicit since they showed Jennifer involved in both oral and vaginal sex with the suspect.

Mrs. Carlson added that Jennifer has refused to talk to her about this problem and has denied any sexual involvement with the suspect even when confronted with the photographs.

I then had Jennifer join her mother and me at the dining table where I tried to question her about the sexual relationship. Jennifer was uncooperative and stated she did not want to talk about what had taken place. She told me that it was her business and none of mine. She stated that she did not feel that she had been victimized at all, and that she was not going to assist in any sort of criminal prosecution or investigation involving the suspect.

I talked with Jennifer for several minutes before she decided to finally disclose some of the sexual involvement between her and the suspect. She would only discuss the sexual activity that was depicted in the six photographs which her mother still had in her possession. Jennifer did identify herself and the suspect as being the people involved in the photographs and that they were taken inside the family home. She stated that the sexual acts "just happened," and she would not elaborate as to the relationship that led up to the photographs being taken or the number of times she was involved sexually with the suspect.

Jennifer stated that if anyone was to blame for the sexual acts, it was her mother, because had her mother been more sexually involved with the suspect, then Jennifer would not have had to substitute for the mother as a lover for the suspect.

Jennifer refused to give any further statement as to her involvement with the suspect. Mrs. Carlson added that she did not know the suspect's current whereabouts, but assumed he was staying in a motel in the general area.

Male Perpetrator - Male Victim

It is quite possible that there are more male victims of child molestation in this age range than female victims. There are a number of reasons that lead me to this opinion, but suffice it to say that there are a lot of male suspects engaging in a lot of sexual activity with underage boys. However, because of society's homosexual stigma to such activities, a lot of these crimes go unreported.

When you do come across such a case, you need to explain to the victim that the actual sexual victimization itself does not mean that they are a homosexual. You have to explain to them that their penis has a "head of its own" and, frequently, it enjoys the sexual contact without understanding the social implications of the male on male activity.

This is especially true of boys who have been victimized over a great length of time, with the molestations beginning when they were approximately 7-to-9-years-old and continuing on into their early teens. When the molestations initially started, they did not attach any sort of homosexual phobias to it, but as they grew older, they began to understand how society views such events. Unfortunately for these kids, once such a sexual relationship develops, it is very difficult for them to get out of that relationship.

Also, in these types of relationships the victim will often have some positive feelings toward the suspect. Many of these victims are seeking some sort of positive influence from an adult, something they are lacking in their home environment. When they find someone who is willing to pay them that positive attention, they frequently end up being victimized by that very person. Since they have no one else in their lives giving them positive input or enhanced self-esteem, they are often reluctant to give up the molester. As stated earlier, you need a combination of victim and suspect profiles for these long-term relationships to continue.

The victim in this type of case has a tendency to diminish the severity of the offense, either by vastly underestimating the number of sexual contacts between him and the suspect or diminishing the severity of them. Sometimes, the child will say they were only fondled, when they had actually been engaged in oral sex. Or, they will say the sexual contact occurred 10 or 20 times, when there were actually several hundred times.

It is also possible that a child in this relationship has been recruiting other children for the offender. Since this type of offender generally prefers children of a certain age range, he has to continually recruit children within that age category. For that reason, it is quite possible that the victim you are talking to was recruited by an older boy at one time and is now recruiting younger children to replace him when he becomes too old for the offender. You need to ask the child about this possibility since you might be able to identify additional victims.

The FBI refers to this as a "pipeline theory." Basically, at one end of the pipeline, you have the offender, who is attracting/recruiting potential victims to him. Normally, this is someone who puts himself in the position to have contact with lots of potential victims, such as a Boy Scout leader or video game arcade operator. As he identifies potential victims, he draws them into the "pipeline," during which time the molestation takes place. During the course of several months or years, the molesting continues until the child becomes too old and, in essence, is deposited on the opposite side of the "pipeline" and discarded because he is no longer sexually attractive to the offender.

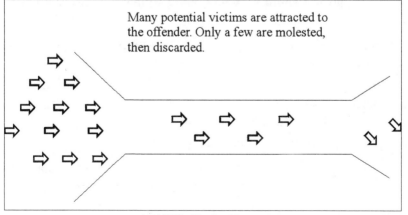

Many potential victims are attracted to the offender. Only a few are molested, then discarded.

(11) FBI's Pipeline Theory

Male Perpetrator - Female Victim

Normally, this involves the dynamic of a male offender having a rather short-term relationship with a female victim. (It can also involve a female suspect and a male victim; the dynamics are usually the same.)

In this type of relationship, the offender normally sees the victim as being much older than their chronological age, and he will see the victim as the sexual aggressor. This offender can be both an in-family and out-of-family perpetrator.

Incest

The law requires that there be actual vaginal intercourse to complete the element of the crime, along with a blood relationship between the suspect and victim. However, the dynamics of the incestuous family, in a clinical sense, would include step-father/daughter relationships, and also sexual acts that only involve oral sex, or sodomy, or fondling.

What happens in an in-family situation like this is that there is a shift in the family structure from what is considered "normal." Basically, there is a realignment of the family structure in which the father becomes closely aligned to the children and the mother is, in essence, an absentee parent. With the absence of the mother as an active participant in the family, a vacuum of sorts is created between the father and the children, which allows them to closely align to each other.

If the father is so inclined to be a child molester, he then will target the children, who are now very vulnerable and accessible to him. The same dynamics can occur with the female/mother as the suspect, but reporting of such incidents is much rarer than the father being the suspect. In such families, both male and female children can be victimized. (Refer to Illustration # 12, page 67.)

In this type of family structure, the child has learned that sex, self-esteem and power are all rolled up together. Because of this, they can be very manipulative within the family and will attempt to manipulate your interview. Sometimes, they won't want to give up the position of power that they have within the family structure, and will downplay the number of times they were involved sexually with the parent.

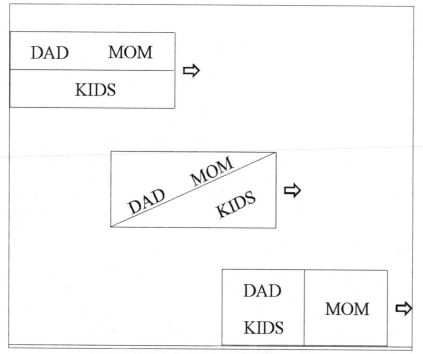

(12) Shift in Family Structure That Leads to Incest

Occasionally you will find a family structure in which the suspect is clinically a rapist, as opposed to a child molester or someone whose sexual preference is actually for children. In this type of situation, the dynamics of the family are dramatically different from that described above. In this type of situation, you will not see a dating-type relationship in which the child is now seen as an age mate to the adult/suspect. The sexual events are more forced and demanded as opposed to coerced and cajoled. The mother is still a nonfunctioning parent within the home and has frequently been so berated by the father that she either fails to see or refuses to see the sexual victimization of her own child.

In this family situation, the child does not have any power within the family structure itself. The child is taught that they have no control over what happens to their body. The child has to submit to the sexual demands of the parent. This causes problems later on in life when this child is now in a dating situation and does not feel powerful enough to say no to the sexual advances of their age mates. This can result in a lot of date rape type scenarios in which the victim did not want to have sex with her date, but she never actively said "no" either.

A family structure with an "in-family rapist" results in a victim with very low self-esteem and a complete blocking of emotions concerning the sexual acts themselves. During an interview of such a child, there may be a complete flat affect with respect to the way she responds to questions about the sexual acts themselves. She may be very "matter-of-fact" about what actually took place. This type of child is not as manipulative as the other in-family victim, since she has not been given any sort of power or pay-back for being involved sexually with the parent. This is also the type of child who will be trying to escape the family environment and will have a history of running away, of committing petty crimes, and other activities that might keep her away from the home.

This type of child basically distrusts all authority figures. She has learned that the parents, who are supposed to protect you in life, actually take advantage of you, so she is not about to trust a stranger to protect her.

In incest and family rape, you have to question the child about sexually explicit photographs being taken of them or shown to them. You also need to ask about any sort of sexual toys or devices that are used during the sexual acts. All of these items are potential evidence to be seized under a search warrant.

Report Narrative: Incest Victim

On 2/02/98, at 0700 hours, I arrived at work. I was contacted by patrol officers, who were speaking with victim #98-020 (Barbara), a 15- year-old female. Patrol personnel told me that they had come into contact with Barbara early this morning. They found her walking down Main Street at about 4:00 a.m. She was visibly upset about something. She told patrol officers that she had run away because her biological father, the suspect, had been molesting her. Patrol officers then brought Barbara to the police department and obtained some basic information from her about the molestation allegation. Patrol requested that I conduct the in-depth interview with her.

I was introduced to Barbara in the Detective Bureau lobby. I took her to the cafeteria area located in the basement of the City Hall building across the courtyard from the police department. At this time of day, the dining area of the cafeteria was empty and I chose to talk with her at a corner table in the cafeteria.

I told Barbara that I was interested in obtaining as much detail as I could about the molestation allegation and that I needed to know this information for various legal reasons. I also told her that the more facts I had, the more I would be able to do for her and help her to prevent this from happening to her again.

By way of background information, Barbara stated that she lives at home with her father, the suspect, and her eight-year-old brother. She said that about four years ago, her mother and father separated and that her alcoholic mother moved out of the home. Barbara has had very limited contact with the mother since that time.

Barbara told me that on her 13th birthday she first had a sexual contact with her father. She told me that on that day, he called her into his bedroom in the early evening hours. He told her that she was old enough to "learn about sex." He told her that he was going to teach her things that she would need to know when she got married. Initially, her father disrobed in front of her and exposed his genitals to her. He then told her that he wanted her to touch his genitals so she would know "what a man feels like." She stated that when she did this, her father's penis became erect. She told me that she was frightened by what was happening, but she did not know what to do to prevent it.

The suspect then told Barbara that she should disrobe in front of him. She told me that she took off all of her clothing except for her panties and bra. At that point, the suspect began to fondle her breasts, telling her that eventually, she would learn to like that type of touching and this was the type of touching that her boyfriends and husband would ultimately do to her. Nothing else happened that night.

Barbara said that two weeks later, her father again called her into his bedroom. At that time, he told her to completely disrobe and he began to fondle her breasts and vaginal area in a skin-to-skin fashion and ultimately masturbated in front of her. He told her it was necessary for her to learn "what happens" during sex, and that is why he masturbated in front of her.

Barbara stated that it was exactly two weeks later when the suspect called her into his bedroom, had her disrobe, and this time had vaginal intercourse with her. She stated that he wore a condom when he did this and told her that she needed to learn about "safe sex." He also told her that as long as he wore a condom, it wasn't like they were actually having intercourse and she would still be considered a virgin.

Barbara said that from that date forward, she had sexual contact with the suspect every other Wednesday night and that it was his routine. Barbara stated that there were *some* special days, however, when the suspect would deviate from the every other Wednesday night pattern. Those days were: the suspect's birthday, Christmas, New Year's and the Fourth of July.

She stated that the suspect told her it was easier for him to have sex with her as opposed to hiring a prostitute or engaging in a dating relationship with an adult female. He told her that it was simply easier for him to have the relationship with her, and it also taught her about sex. The suspect said that someday she would be thankful for his instruction in this area.

According to Barbara, the regular sexual activity has been consistent for the past two years. Because of that, she has run away from home several times over the last few months in an attempt to escape her father. However, each time she has gone back home because she did not know where else to go. She also told me that she did not think anyone would believe her if she were to tell them what was happening at home.

Barbara told me that she ran away the previous night rather than have sex with her father. She told me that she climbed out of her bedroom window shortly after dinner to escape from being called to his bedroom to have sex with him.

Barbara went on to state that every time she had vaginal intercourse with the suspect, he always wore a condom and that he kept a supply of condoms in the night stand near his bed.

Barbara also stated that several times he had shown her sexually explicit photographs from adult magazines. He would suggest that they engage in the type of sexual activity depicted on the magazine pages. Specifically, he was making reference to oral and anal sex. Barbara was reluctant to engage in these activities and the suspect never forced them on her. She stated that each time they had intercourse, she would just lie on her back on top of his bed and the intercourse would take perhaps two to three minutes.

I returned to the Detective Bureau with Barbara. I called Records and found out that the suspect had reported his daughter as a runaway last night. I also found three prior runaway reports on her.

I told Barbara I was interested in her making a clandestine telephone call to the suspect. I explained the nature of the call, that being that she should attempt to solicit statements from him that would amount to admissions to his sexual involvement with her. I told her she would have to be very specific to be sure that we were talking about a *sexual* relationship between her and the suspect, as opposed to any other type of relationship. I spent about fifteen minutes explaining the nature and procedure for the call, and Barbara stated she was willing to do so.

I went into the "cold room" inside the Narcotic Unit. The "cold room" is set up with a telephone where a conversation can be monitored and recorded. I called my own extension at the police department to test the equipment. I listed the case number, date and time of the call as well as the nature of it. (*NOTE*: You should always play the recording back to make sure your equipment is working and check your own state's laws regarding the recording of phone conversations.)

I then asked Barbara to join me in the "cold room." After I dialed the suspect's telephone number, I handed the phone to her, placing the headphones on my head so I could listen to both sides of the conversation while it was being taped.

When the suspect answered the phone, Barbara identified herself and stated that she was calling from a friend's house and that she only had a few minutes to talk. The suspect asked her why she had run away again, and she responded by stating she ran away because she did not want to have sex with him anymore. The call lasted approximately ten to fifteen minutes, during which the suspect repeatedly stated that the reason he was having sex with her was because it was better for the family that he do so, as opposed to him having a girlfriend that would take him away from the family.

During the call, she stated several times that she did not want to have sexual intercourse with him anymore, nor was she interested in engaging in other sexual acts that he continued to show her via the adult magazines. The suspect said that if she was really serious about not wanting to have sex with him, they could discuss it if she would return home. Barbara told him that she did not know if she was going to come home and, at my direction, she ended the call by hanging up on him.

I made arrangements for Barbara to be taken into protective custody and prepared a search warrant for the suspect's residence in order to obtain the condoms and the sexually explicit magazines described by Barbara.

Female Perpetrators - Female Victims

This is probably the *least reported* type of sexual victimization. In the few cases I have handled, I have seen the same dynamics as in male suspects and female victims since the victim suffers the same loss of self-esteem, ability to trust and suffers from fear of reprisal or disapproval from the victimizer or from society. This type of victimization occurs to victims ranging from infancy through late teens. When interviewing the victim or suspect in this type of case, you simply need to understand the dynamics of the relationship, as in all cases, and your interview is the same as it would be where there is a male suspect and male victim. The same rules and techniques should be applied in both situations and as set out in the next paragraph.

Female Perpetrators - Male Victims

Adult females having sex with underage males is a crime that is vastly underreported. This is due to the duality in thinking (a double standard) in America that if a female is a victim of a sexual assault, it needs to be reported and someone needs to be prosecuted, but if an adult female has sex with a young boy, it is unfortunately considered by most to be a passage into manhood.

Because of this double standard, many of these types of crimes do not get reported. Frequently society sees a teenage boy who is having sex with an adult female as being "lucky," and that this type of relationship is his passage into manhood. However, California law is very clear that such relationships are criminal in the same sense as if the sexes were reversed. California Penal Code Section 261.5, Unlawful Intercourse With a Person Under 18 Years, was made gender neutral several years ago. (See your individual state laws.)

When interviewing such a male victim, you should do so in the same fashion as you would a female victim.

The "Mrs. Robinson Syndrome" has been romanticized in our culture. *Summer of '42* and *Private Lessons* are other film examples of glorifying the exploitation of a young male by an adult female. However, the traumatic effect on a victim of such a crime can be devastating and the long-term results of this victimization can be severe. In several of the books listed in the bibliography, you will see that some of the most savage sex criminals were childhood victims of female perpetrators.

Female child molesters can "get by" with a lot of inappropriate sexual touching of very young children during bath time and helping them dress, etc., which would be dismissed as "care-taking" or "nurturing" activity if disclosed by the child. Yet if the same acts were committed by a man, they would be suspect. The key ingredient to determining if a sex crime has been committed *is that the perpetrator committed the acts for their own gratification, not for the benefit of the child nor with any regard for the impact it would have on the child.* In a clinical sense, these types of suspects can be fixated or regressed offenders, they can be rapists, they can operate within their own family or they can operate outside of the family, even assaulting strangers.

As the male child victim becomes older and the sexual contact becomes more involved, you have a sexual victimization of the male child by the adult female with the same dynamics as any other child molestation situation.

When an adult female is involved sexually with a teenage boy, the victim is often considered as "being lucky" to have a female adult teach him about sex. In reality, what is happening is that he is being sexually victimized the same as if he were being assaulted by a male suspect. If the roles were reversed and an adult male were having sex with a teenage female there would be no doubt in anybody's mind that it is wrong, and a crime is being committed. Society tends to condone this type of behavior and, as a result, the victim is compelled to suppress his feelings about the victimization, or if he does report, he is discounted and the severity of the impact of the incident diminished, often by those in positions of authority.

Generally speaking, men tend to express their negative feelings through anger. When a man feels anxiety, helplessness, loneliness, etc., he tends to try to express these feelings through angry behavior or by being "macho." In extreme cases, this anger is ultimately projected by the man, and in an attempt to displace all of these feelings and somehow relieve the tremendous feeling of low self-esteem, he strikes out in anger and then becomes, himself, a perpetrator, often a violent one.

Some experts believe that if a man has been emotionally, physically or sexually abused by a female, he will have a tendency to hate women in general because they are the cause of all of his bad feelings. He then tries to "get even" for all of these wrongs that have been done to him. It is through the projection of the anger that the adult male who was a child victim attempts to "get even." If he has learned to eroticize violence, you are now looking at the profile of a rapist. If that victim has not learned to eroticize violence, he may be someone who is continually getting into fights, even to the extreme of committing assaults with a deadly weapon—and even murders. In the mid-eighties a study was conducted at San Quentin which found that 100% of those incarcerated for violent crimes had been victims of child abuse. This is a significant fact to keep in mind before you discount any child's account of abuse of any nature.

I have spoken with several teenage boys who have been sexually assaulted by females. Many of them expressed tremendous fear and confusion about what was happening to them. They felt a complete lack of control over their bodies during the assaults and experienced great feelings of conflict and guilt about the incidents. If a male child is allowed to express those feelings and deal with them, as female victims are encouraged to do, then they will be able to cope with the victimization and move on with their life. However, as with all traumatic feeling suppression, there is a potential for disaster with regard to a person eventually acting out their anger and they could become a sexual predator. Lacking any sense of control in their own life, they attempt to use sexual assault as an opportunity to be in control.

Example: Adult Female Perpetrator - Adolescent Male Victim

Several years ago I investigated a case which profoundly displays the double standard thinking. A patrol officer found a parked car behind a closed industrial complex late one night. The seats were reclined in the vehicle and it appeared that he had stumbled across a couple of "lovers." When the officer approached the vehicle, he found a fourteen-year-old boy, completely naked, sitting behind the wheel. Sitting next to him was a forty-year-old female teacher who was fully clothed. As soon as the officer approached the car, the female jumped out and spontaneously stated, "We didn't have time to do anything. We were going to do something sexual, but we didn't have time. You caught us too soon; we didn't do anything wrong." The officer was told that the boy's clothes were in the trunk, at which time he allowed the boy to retrieve his clothing and dress. While dressing, more information of what happened was revealed.

The schoolteacher stated that she was tutoring the boy and he snuck out of his house (at midnight) to meet her down the street from his residence. This was their normal routine. The female allowed the boy to drive her car (a privilege which is not uncommon for a pedophile to offer in exchange for the sexual activity) and they had gone somewhere to obtain something to eat. According to the female, the boy then spilled his meal onto his lap and had to remove all of his clothing and place it into the trunk of the car "because they would dry faster in the trunk than in the passenger compartment." (Sometimes it is hard for an officer to keep a straight face!) The officer learned that the boy's parents were aware of the relationship and had been trying to stop it for several months. However, they had been unsuccessful and the boy kept sneaking out at night and meeting with the teacher for this "special tutoring."

The officer told the schoolteacher that she would have to drive the car since the boy was unlicensed and that she should immediately take the boy home to his parents. He let them drive away and handled the whole incident on a field interview card.

When the situation was called to my attention, I contacted the school and learned that the teacher had been warned numerous times to stay away from not only this particular boy, but several others with whom she had been in contact over the last several years. The school administration had a requirement that she never close her classroom door and that she had been forbidden to work in a one-on-one situation with any of her male pupils because she had a tendency to "be too close" to her male students. (See "Mobile Molester" in the Advocacy section.)

Holding the entire incident up to scrutiny, if the schoolteacher had been a male, and the fourteen-year-old been a female, a whole different outcome would have occurred. Obviously, the schoolteacher would have been arrested, the parents of the child would have been contacted to come pick up their daughter and criminal charges would have been filed—the double standard was certainly in effect.

I am sure there are some of you reading this, both male and female, who have some doubt as to whether or not the female schoolteacher "teaching" her pupil about sex was inappropriate and fail to see the potential traumatic effect it might have on the boy.

Think for a moment of how vulnerable you were at the age of twelve. Imagine being that age and being the constant unwilling sexual partner of your stepmother. Think of how you would feel every night, going to bed knowing that your stepmother would come in drunk at two or three in the morning and demand some type of sexual acts. *That scenario is a passage into terror, not a passage into manhood.* Compounding the impact is that while the male child may be dreading the moment the stepmother arrives, and experiencing remorse about the betrayal of his father, he finds himself lying in bed with a full erection. Aroused sex organs have no conscience—especially when a male is eleven or twelve. Conflicts with no possible solutions create mental imbalance. Hopefully, this helps you understand why such a male child victim could become such a violent adult.

Clandestine Telephone Calls from Victims

Victims of this age range are good candidates for making clandestine telephone calls to the suspects. They are old enough to understand the nature of the call, that being to solicit incriminating statements from the suspect. This type of call is only successful if the perpetrator is unaware that the child has come to the police department to report the offenses.

Date Rape

Females between the ages of thirteen and eighteen are prime candidates for date rape, or acquaintance rape scenarios. Because of the normal irresponsible behaviors of adolescents, they frequently get themselves into situations that they cannot get themselves out of. Often, they will either be hitchhiking or come in contact with a stranger when they are intoxicated or have been using drugs. Because of this, they find themselves being victimized quite routinely.

Suspects who commit such rapes are predators in the same sense as the person who commits a stranger-type abduction and rape. However, their choice of victims are those who are more vulnerable to attack because of their age and/or degree of intoxication.

Being the victim of this type of offense has an additional traumatizing effect to the victim since it attacks her ability to choose safe people to be around. So, in addition to the violation of the body and her ability to be in control of her body, she also now has to question her ability to choose safe friends.

Sex of Interviewer

My experience has been that it doesn't make any difference as to whether or not a male or female interviews any sexual assault victim. What is more important are the abilities of the individual interviewer/officer. I have seen some females who are very good interviewers; and I have seen some who are absolutely horrible. The same is true for male officers. To routinely think that a female victim would automatically feel more comfortable talking to a female officer is erroneous. There is also a school of thought that teaches a male officer might be the best to interview a female victim since it will help her to regain a feeling/sense that men are safe to be around after she has been victimized by a male. The concept of *Strength Through Association* will be discussed in more detail in subsequent chapters.

The most important quality of interviewing a victim is your ability to portray a professional image toward the victim. This professional need-to-know, no-nonsense image allows you to ask all of the sensitive, pertinent sexual questions that you need to know to fulfill your crime reporting requirements.

Stranger Rape

(Refer to Chapter 5 regarding Adult Victims.)

Medical Exams

Because many of these sexual offenses are accomplished with the threat of force or while the victim is unable to resist because of intoxication, often the only physical evidence will be found during the medical exam. (Refer to the Chapter 5 on Adult Victimization for further details.)

False Reports

In this age range, there are numerous reasons why someone might falsely report a rape. Many of these false reports are simply attempts to redirect attention away from something wrong that the victim has done so that he/she is not disciplined for coming home late, joy-riding in the family car, some sort of drug use, or violation of other household rules. Sometimes the victim who has committed a violation of household rules will make up a story about being sexually assaulted in order to gain sympathy for the sexual assault, as opposed to being disciplined for violating household rules.

Other motivations for a false report would be someone who had a consensual sexual act but is afraid that they have now contracted a venereal disease or become pregnant and needed to explain the pregnancy or sexually transmitted disease to their family.

Fortunately, victims in this age range are not very sophisticated in coming up with a story about being victimized, and a detailed interview with them will reveal several discrepancies or holes in their story that will normally indicate if their report is false.

THIS PAGE INTENTIONALLY LEFT BLANK

CHAPTER 5

INTERVIEWING AGES 18 - 80

Generally, victims in this age range are thought of as being one-time kidnap and rape victims, or victims or random sexual assault as opposed to an ongoing type of victimization that you see with children. (The only exception to this would be in spousal abuse/rape cases which will be discussed later.)

When The Suspect Is A Stranger

First contact

In this type of case, generally the first contact with the victim is via the 911 emergency line where she or a friend has called in to report the sexual assault. The 911 tape is a critical evidence item. The spontaneous statements exception to the hearsay rule in the California Evidence Code allows such 911 tapes, along with spontaneous statements made to witnesses immediately after the assault, to be used as evidence.(See your individual state codes.) You should request from your communications supervisor that a copy of the 911 tape be maintained for evidence.

Also, be sure to contact any "fresh complaint" witnesses. This could include a husband, boyfriend, parent, or anyone that the victim contacted prior to actually calling the police department. Also, emergency room nurses and doctors can fall within this exception to the hearsay rule as "fresh complaint witnesses." If the victim makes a spontaneous statement to them, this can be used in court to help corroborate her statement.

Stalking

Generally speaking, sexual predators do not follow one particular victim for an extended length of time prior to committing a sexual assault. Although I am sure it does happen on rare occasions, generally speaking, the sexual predator does not have the impulse control to delay immediate gratification of his needs for several months or years. It would be extremely rare for one victim to be stalked by a total stranger for an extended length of time for the purpose of sexual assault or for repeated sexual assaults by the same suspect. The classical stalker is generally obsessed with an individual for other than sexual reasons. Usually their obsession stems from broken romances to problems in the workplace or even celebrities.

Predator Rapist

In general terms, the rapist/sexual predator is seeking to level a balance beam scale in his head. When the scale is balanced, he acts normally and does not assault. As he starts to get out of tilt because of some real or perceived wrongs in his life, he begins to fantasize about raping someone, which gives him a feeling of power, which helps balance the scale. As he becomes increasingly out of kilter, he begins to act out on his fantasies.

The associated fantasy is that the suspect will assault a woman and this sexual experience will be overwhelmingly positive for both the suspect and the victim and that both the suspect and the victim will fall madly in love with each other and they will ride off into the sunset together and live happily ever after. Unfortunately for the suspect, this never happens. The victim never falls madly in love with him and frequently the suspect has difficulty maintaining an erection or actually achieving ejaculation.

The rape does satisfy the need for power, control and domination over the victim, but does not satisfy a basic sexual need, as most of society would see it. As a result, the suspect sees the victim as having failed, since she was not sexy enough, involved enough in the sexual assault, or there was something wrong with the victim that caused the fantasy to be unfulfilled.

Because of this combination of fantasy versus balancing the power/emotion scale in the suspect's head, it would be very unlikely for a suspect to follow and continually sexually assault the same victim over and over again because *she* has failed to fulfill his fantasy.

Also, the unbalancing of the emotional scale inside the suspect's head happens very quickly. For that reason, he needs an immediate solution to his dilemma, that being his inability to deal with his own emotions. As a result, he will basically grab a victim of convenience or opportunity.

What is more likely to take place is that a rapist, when the scales are slightly out of whack, will start to prowl the neighborhood in which he lives. This kind of suspect finds large apartment complexes the same as shopping malls for him, since he will continually prowl the complex to look for victims. He will know every open window; he will know every female who lives in those apartment; he will know when they are alone and when their husbands are at home; he will know every crack in the venetian blinds that he can peek through to get a glimpse of a potential victim.

Generally, this peeking and prowling process helps stabilize the emotional teeter totter in his head since the fantasy about being able to break in and rape the victim will, most times, satisfy the emotional need for power and control over the victim. It is only when the scale is tipped drastically that he actually acts out on the fantasy and breaks into the apartment and rapes.

It is more likely that your average rapist has a general idea of many potential victims in the immediate area where he lives. If he finds the need on a particular night to act out on the sexual fantasy, he will know which victim he can go to on that particular date and time, since he will know who is available, and he can go in and assault them at that time.

This same type of suspect, when he finds the need to fantasize about controlling a woman, might prowl the freeways or the super-market parking lots for potential victims. This is the type of person who will see a potential victim driving alone on the freeway and will start following her for an extended length of time. He will follow her and fantasize about being able to rape her. If he actually follows her to her home, he might wait outside for a while, again fantasizing about the rape and, in essence, working up the nerve to carry out the sexual assault. He may then approach the victim with some sort of a ruse, such as knocking on the door and claiming to be the TV repairman, or the man from the Gas Company, etc. to make entry and then capture the victim and follow through with the sexual assault.

He may also find a victim he is attracted to at the supermarket and may follow her home and assault her in a similar fashion.

Because of this, it is important to obtain background information from the victim as to what their activities were prior to the sexual assault, going back at least several hours prior to the actual capture by the suspect. You might want to go back 24 hours through the victim's routine and find out if sometime during that 24 hours, there might have been a time when she came into contact with the suspect.

If the attack occurs in a neighborhood or apartment complex where the victim has lived for some time, you should ask her if she is aware of any complaints from other neighbors about people peeking in their windows or theft of lingerie from the laundry rooms. You should also make contact with the apartment manager to see if they are aware of similar complaints. The manager may also be aware of prowlers or other nuisance crimes that the victim is not aware of.

Since rape involves the control of the victim by the suspect, it would not be unusual for a suspect to break into an unoccupied residence where a female lives by herself and, in essence, control her property by stealing her underwear or being inside her bedroom where he can fantasize about being able to rape her if she had actually been home. He might go so far as to masturbate over her bed or onto her clothing. The apartment managers may be aware of these types of crimes occurring within the complex prior to the actual rape of the victim that you are interviewing.

There are several different types of rapists, as defined by Dr. Nicholas Groth and others. Refer to the bibliography for further readings in this area.

Modus Operandi vs. Fantasy of Rapist

Modus operandi (or MO) generally refers to the method in which a suspect robs a bank or breaks into a house to commit a burglary. Generally, in those types of crimes, you don't have to go beyond the MO to help you identify the motivating factor in the crime, that being obtaining money. However, in sex offenses, the MO is considerably different from that of a property crime.

In a sex offense, MO is that tactic, or technique, that brings the suspect into contact with the victim. These approaches can be as ingenious as calling an escort service to his house, using a dating service to make contact with females, placing some sort of drug into a woman's drink at a nightclub in order to get her to accompany him someplace, or it could be as basic as breaking into her home, holding a gun to her head and raping her, or kidnapping her off the street at knife-point.

Once the suspect has been successful in capturing the female, then the secondary phase of the assault takes place, and this is the actual fantasy phase in which the suspect acts out the fantasy as to how he wants the assault to take place. The fantasies can be very basic or they can be quite elaborate.

Sexual Assault Phases

Everything the suspect does during the actual assault phase means something to him. It may not mean anything to you, the interviewer, but it has great importance to the suspect. With that in mind, if the victim tells you something that seems rather bizarre, be sure to document it because it is very important in identifying the suspect later on. If possible, during your investigation, you should try to identify the following phases of the sexual assault. These are:

A. The approach phase - This may involve following the victim home from the supermarket, prowling her apartment complex, or meeting her in a bar.

B. Contact - The suspect may confront her at knife-point in the carports, break into the residence and confront her in bed, or pull a weapon on a hitchhiker or prostitute who willingly got into the car with the suspect.

C. Capture - The capture of the victim is actually complete once she decides to submit to the sexual assault, as opposed to being killed or physically injured by the suspect. Perhaps 70% of suspects will only use enough force necessary to actually capture the victim.

There are suspects who actually enjoy inflicting physical pain to the victim, and these are the ones who use an excessive amount of force to continually beat or stab the victim far beyond that necessary to capture her for the purposes of the sexual assault.

D. Assault phase - This is the actual sexual assault itself and may include a great deal of dialog by the suspect directing the victim to do or say certain things during the rape.

E. Post-assault behavior - During this phase, the suspect will sometimes be apologetic to the victim, often trying to explain to her why he needed to rape her, thereby justifying his action. These excuses are normally lies, but they usually consist of statements such as, "My girlfriend just broke up with me," or, "My girlfriend is pregnant and I haven't had sex in a long time." It is not unusual in a post-assault phase for the suspect to get the victim something to drink, ask her for her telephone number, carry on some general conversation with her, or perhaps tell her how to better secure her house in the future so that no one else can break in.

F. Escape phase - This is when the suspect actually terminates contact with the victim and flees. In a burglary rape situation, it is not unusual for him to have prepared his exit prior to his actually using it, e.g., he will break in through a window, but prior to making contact with the victim, he will unlock the front door so he can leave immediately.

He may have a vehicle parked nearby to help aid in his escape or, if he lives nearby, he will simply flee on foot. Identifying his escape route is often very import as far as finding physical evidence that might lead to his identity.

Age of Victim

Most suspects are very opportunistic in their selection of victims. Basically, when they feel the need to rape, they will grab a victim of opportunity providing a wide age range in which they will sexually assault. Since the suspect sees the victim as an entity to possess, as opposed to a real person, he really doesn't care about the age of the victim. I have seen the same suspect attack victims between the ages of 11 and 80, all of the women being victims of opportunity.

However, due to the emotional make-up of these suspects, a lot of them do not feel very adequate when dealing with women. Sometimes, you will see a suspect in this category who will only assault very young children and/or the elderly. Both of these groups, young children and the elderly, are seen as non-sexual beings. Since society generally does not think of children as having any sort of sexual knowledge or experiences, the suspect does not have to perform adequately for this child and, as a result, he can assault them without a fear of being laughed at because of his inability to satisfy the victim. Also in our society, grandmothers are not considered to be sexual beings and for that reason, the same suspect who is raping children, may see an elderly victim as being a non-sexual person for whom he does not have to perform adequately. For this reason, he may assault this population group also.

Perpetrator's Rape Kits

Sometimes, suspects will prepare a rape kit to take with them on their sexual assault adventures. This will involve a backpack or duffel bag that will contain tools they may need to use in order to accomplish the rape. You may find a ski mask, gloves, duct tape, handcuffs, guns, knives, pry tools, etc. in this rape kit that may be carried around by the suspect to help him in capturing a victim. To some suspects, the actual acquiring of these items is a part of the fantasy and, in essence, a part of the "date" prior to the sexual assault. Some of them carry the rape kit around with them to help them fantasize about raping a woman of opportunity. It helps them with the fantasy process to know that they have the tools available to them to commit a sexual assault if they choose to do so.

Rapists are masters at fantasizing. They have taken the ability to fantasize in order to stabilize the balance beam in their head to an absolute extreme. Anything that aids them in this fantasy, such as the rape kit, will help them in balancing the emotional scale in their head.

Keep in mind that just because a person is a rapist (or a child molester), it does not exclude him from being another kind of criminal also. The rapist can be a bank robber, a burglar, can write bad checks, be a drug user, or all of the above. When investigating these types of crimes, if you were to come across a "rape kit", or any other items that might make you believe the person you are dealing with is a rapist, be sure to take those items of evidence, or at least document them and see to it that the sex crimes investigators are aware of who this person is so that they might link him to unsolved crimes.

Rape Trauma Syndrome

The emotional and physical symptoms experienced by rape victims have been analyzed and assembled into a group called the Rape Trauma Syndrome. (Refer to Appendix "A".)

The initial response to being sexually assaulted is a denial of the emotional impact of the assault on the victim. Because of this, a lot of victims will show a very flat or negative affect when you initially approach them. The victim may be upset and crying when you first arrive, but once she realizes that she is safe with you, don't be alarmed if she shuts off all expressions of emotion and becomes very easy to interview.

Since the victim will probably want to deny the emotional impact of the assault, it makes for an easy interview because they will become very matter-of-fact during the interview process itself. However, when you get to the actual sexual assault, i.e., the actual vaginal penetration, or the actual initiation of oral sex, often the memory of that act overpowers them and, once again, they will break down and start to cry or visibly shake. Be sure to document these emotions during your police report because *you* have now become a spontaneous statement witness and, per the exception to the Evidence Code, you can now testify as to the victim's emotional state at the time you contacted them.

Interview: Rape Victim

Normally, in a one-time rape situation when you are called immediately to the location, you, as a police officer, will contain the initial crime scene, have additional officers set up a perimeter, and then conduct a crime scene search for evidence and obtain a suspect description. This process is exactly the same as it would be for any sort of in-progress or recently committed crime that you might respond to.

In the sexual assault, however, you normally want to get the victim to a hospital where you can be sure her medical needs are being taken care of. Often, the interview with the victim takes place at the hospital while you are waiting for the doctor to be available to examine her.

In this type of situation, the victim is very much aware of why you are there and is aware that you are going to interview her about what took place. Explain to the victim that you are going to spend a lot of time talking to her, but that you are going to spend *most* of the time talking about what led up to the actual sexual assault, this being the approach, contact, and capture phase, as opposed to spending a great deal of time on the actual sexual assault itself. Tell her that you are very interested in what the suspect said during the time they were in contact with each other and in what his post-assault behaviors were. This allows the victim to relax a little bit, since she won't have to spend hours talking about the actual physical penetration of her body, which is normally what the public fears the police interview in a rape situation involves.

You have to convey to the victim that you have a *legitimate need* to know the information that you are going to be asking and to assure her that you are not going to go back to the station and talk about her victimization as if you had just seen an X-rated movie. Once the victim feels comfortable in talking to you, the interview is generally quite easy.

After relaying basic suspect information to assisting officers, you need to settle into the long-term interviewing process with the victim. You can start off by asking the victim what she has done in the last several hours, i.e., if she has returned home from a date, if she was at the supermarket, if she returned directly home from work, or if she had just gotten up in the morning, etc. This eases you into the interview process and gives you the information you might need as to where she has been and where she might have first been observed by the suspect.

Keep in mind that the victim may not be aware of the first time that the suspect actually observed her. For that reason, you want to advise her of this and simply tell her that it is possible that the suspect followed her home, or possibly someone in the neighborhood that she hasn't thought of as a potential suspect. During this interview process, she may suddenly realize that there was someone who contacted her several hours earlier at the market or was following her home on the freeway and she has not made the connection between that initial contact and the sexual assault.

When questioning her about the first contact between her and the suspect, you need to find out what physically happened, such as he broke in through a window, or he knocked on the front door and pretended to be a repairman, or he approached her on the sidewalk with a gun in his hand. But you also need to ask her what his demeanor was like. Ask her if he was in a heightened stage of anxiety, if he was breathing heavily, if he was apologetic or very angry, and at what point in time this demeanor changed, if it did, during the contact he had with her. Frequently, a suspect will be in a state of very high anxiety at the time he makes initial contact with the victim, but once he has been successful in capturing her, he may become more relaxed. What the victim might mistake as being a relaxed state is more likely the suspect entering the fantasy phase of the rape scenario.

You also need to ask the victim if the suspect only used enough force to successfully capture her. One of the elements of a forcible rape is that the suspect overcame any resistance by the victim by using force, fear, or the threat of great bodily injury. You need to obtain details from the victim that fulfills this element of the crime. Basically, if the victim tells you that she was afraid she was going to be killed because the suspect put a gun in her face and said he would kill her if she did not comply, then obviously that fulfills that element. Often, the simple size difference between the suspect and victim is enough for her to feel this fear element and a need to comply out of fear of being severely beaten by the suspect.

It is important to explain to the victim that every time a sexual act took place, that a separate and distinct crime has occurred. If the suspect initially inserts a finger into the victim's vagina, that is a separate felony. If he then performed oral sex on her, that is also a separate felony. If she performed oral sex on him, that is another separate felony. If he has intercourse with her, that is also a separate felony. Each time a different felony is committed, these crimes can be charged separately against the suspect and he is sentenced separately on each act. Most sexual assaults involve several felonies perpetrated on the victim. In an average rape case, the suspect may have committed several individual sexual assaults on the victim in addition to, perhaps, kidnapping or falsely imprisoning her, or using a firearm during the course of the assault which may result in an enhanced sentence. You need to explain to the victim that the reason you want the details about the sexual assault is so you can document each of these individual crimes so that the suspect's prison sentence will increase with each crime.

Once the victim understands this, she should have no problem in telling you what took place. Occasionally, she will be upset with having had to perform a sexual act that she finds is particularly distasteful, and you need to be sensitive to her feelings. But generally speaking, they will be very forthright with what took place.

If a victim is having difficulty remembering the sequence of events as they unfolded during the assault phase, you may want to interview her starting from the last contact with the perpetrator, working backward in time. You explain this to her by saying that it might be very easy for her to recite the alphabet from A through Z, but if she were to try to recite the alphabet backwards, from Z to A, she would have to stop and think about each letter as she was going backwards to be sure that she got it in the proper sequence. The same thing is true for recalling the actual sexual assault itself if she is a little confused about which event happened first. If you can take her backwards through the event, sometimes it forces her to think about them in a little more detail and you can get a little clearer picture as to what took place.

There is no real reason to "overkill" the actual sexual acts themselves. If the victim tells you that the suspect had an erection and placed his erect penis into her vagina, that satisfies the elements of the crime. If you can get an approximate length of time the intercourse took place, such as two minutes, three minutes, five minutes, etc., that's fine, but it isn't overly important as far as the actual elements of a crime are concerned. The same thing holds true for rape with a foreign object. If the suspect puts one finger inside of the victim's vagina, two fingers, or three fingers, it really doesn't change the elements of the crime any. If the victim can recall if it was one or two fingers, that's fine, but don't belabor these types of points with them. I have seen many interviewers get so tied up in trying to figure out whether the suspect put one or two fingers inside of the victim, that it became burdensome to the point of being absurd.

I have also seen interviewers go on at great length to try to ascertain if the victim knew if the suspect ejaculated. Whether or not a suspect ejaculated during the vaginal intercourse with the victim is not an element of the crime. It has absolutely no importance as far as the law is concerned. It does have some importance as to finding biological evidence that might help identify the suspect, but that is really its only importance.

Since the suspect ejaculating is only important as far as collecting physical evidence is concerned, you should explain this to the victim and then ask her where the biological evidence might be, such as on her clothing or inside her body, on the bedding, on the car seat or on the floor.

If the suspect is having difficulty maintaining an erection during the sexual assault, you need to document this in as much detail as possible. You need to correspond his lack of being able to maintain an erection with what did he do to resolve that problem, such as masturbate himself, or have the victim perform oral sex on him, and what his demeanor or mood was like at these times. Did he become apologetic? Did he become angry?

The victims ability to explain the suspect's actions, demeanor, and words used as the assault is continuing, is very helpful in discovering what his fantasy is. Most suspects will act out the same fantasy several times and then after four or five sexual assaults, the fantasy will change somewhat.

Since we know that MO and fantasy are two separate things, it is quite possible that a particular suspect will come into contact with victims in a different fashion. If a rape suspect has an MO that is working for him, he will try to stay with it. But the opportunistic nature of this type of individual may result in a momentary change in MO/contact. Just because a suspect breaks into a house and confronts a victim in her bed at 3:00 a.m., puts a knife to her throat and rapes her, doesn't mean that he won't also rape a hitchhiker, or that he won't rape a prostitute, or a woman working for an out-call service who comes to his house. He may have several different MOs that bring him in contact with potential victims. However, the fantasy that he acts out once he has captured the victim will quite often be the same or very similar.

It is very helpful in identifying suspects who have committed multiple offenses through the fantasy if the patrol officer can try to detail the mood and terminology used during the sexual assault. For example, he might call the victim a "bitch" or a "whore" while she is performing oral sex on him, but when he is performing vaginal intercourse with her, he may want her to repeat phrases like, "You're the best lover I've every had," or, "You have the biggest penis I've ever had." This is very important terminology for identifying offenders later on.

It is not unusual for a suspect, after he has captured a victim, to appear as if he is reading from a script as the sexual assault goes on. Frequently, the suspect has fantasized the rape scenario over and over so many times in his mind that he wants it to occur specifically as he has rehearsed it. If you can elicit from the victim as to whether or not the suspect went into a phase where it appeared he was reading from an invisible script, this may be very helpful in identifying who he is later on.

Male vs. Female Interviewers

It has been my experience that the sex of the interviewer has absolutely no bearing on the quality of information obtained from the victim. What is more important is the interviewer's ability to establish a rapport and the serious approach required to obtain the information from the victim. There is also a school of thought that says that a male interviewer talking to a female rape victim is very therapeutic for the female. This allows the female to have a safe contact with a male who is in a position of power, who is not going to victimize her, which begins the process of rebuilding her ability to trust men. This *Strength Through Association* helps start the recovery process and helps build rapport between the officer and the victim.

Obviously, if you have a rape victim who wishes to be interviewed by a female officer, by all means do what you can to oblige her request. However, it has been my experience that this really is not a problem and most victims feel perfectly comfortable talking to a male about the sexual assault, as long as it is done properly.

False Rape Reports

False reporting of rapes is a bigger problem than most people realize. It has become such a problem that the FBI has developed a profile of the person who falsely reports a sexual assault. A copy of that profile is attached in Appendix "B" and should be reviewed by the reader at this time.

I have encountered many fictitious rapes that can be listed in several broad categories, as listed below. This does not mean that any rape that has some of these characteristics is a false report. Some of the motivating factors I have come across are:

A. Intoxication: This is when a female becomes so intoxicated by drugs and/or alcohol that she wakes up with the "wrong guy."

B. Pregnant/STD: This is when a female fears she has become pregnant or has contracted a sexually transmitted disease during consensual sex, but is afraid to tell her parents, boyfriend or husband how "it" actually happened.

C. Attention: This type is seeking attention, not only from the police department, but from friends and relatives. People who fall into this category often have elaborate stories about having been stalked by the suspect for an extended length of time. They are also notorious for "late" reporting their sexual victimization. This is also the type of person who would be more likely to self-inflict injuries to corroborate her allegation of rape.

D. Misdirection: This type diverts attention away from some violation of household rules (normally a teenager violating curfew). She will state that the reason she came home late was because she was raped, gaining sympathy from her parents instead of being punished.

E. Homeward Bound: This victim has moved out of her family's home to be "on her own," but finds that it is too difficult. However she doesn't want to admit this, so she fabricates a rape, normally occurring in her new apartment, in order to get the family to "force" her to return home.

F. Broken Lease: In order to break a rental agreement, the victim will report that someone has broken into her home and sexually assaulted her. She then tells that landlord that she is too fearful to live there any longer and needs to be allowed to get out of the lease agreement. A variation of this is when the rent money has been spent on drugs and the victim reports that someone broke into the apartment stole the rent money and raped her. This allows her to not pay the upcoming month's rent and then break the lease.

G. Sympathy/Guilt: These victims have recently broken up with a boyfriend or husband and will report that they were assaulted to gain a sympathy or guilt reaction. When successful, the ex-mate will come running back to protect her from the rapist.

H. Cheating Wife: This woman is having an affair and has in essence "overslept" and does not return home on time. She will fictitiously report a rape to account for her time away from home. This also "covers" any pregnancy or STD she may have acquired.

I. Copycat: This type is similar to the attention seeker and surfaces during a series of legitimate rapes that have received a lot of news media attention. This woman will report that she too has been attacked by the same cat burglar or stalker. This is another reason why it is important to carefully document the statements made by the suspect during the capture and assault phases of the legitimate rapes. You then have to keep this information away from the news media so it is not commonly known. This way, when the copycat victim surfaces, she will not be able to tell a story that is consistent with the other, legitimate, victims.

J. Mentally Ill: This category has several sub-categories.

1. Extremely Mentally Disturbed Case: This person has extreme form(s) of mental illness which causes her to fictitiously report a rape or other crime.

2. Emotion Turmoil: This person needs to reach out for some sort of psychological help but doesn't know how to do so in a more legitimate fashion. They need to escape from the source of stress in their lives so they make up a rape story that allows them to do so, without "losing face" to their family and friends. An example of this would be a college student who is under a tremendous amount of pressure from herself and family to be a very high achiever. If the pressure from this high performance becomes overwhelming, she will fabricate a rape or stalker in order to allow her to flee the academic environment in order to get away from the attacker. This is very similar to the HOMEWARD BOUND type.

   When dealing with these people, you have to be careful not to "push them over the edge." Because of their mental instability, being confrontational (calling them a liar) might cause them to commit suicide. You might suggest that they seek counseling for the "rape." A good counselor will be able to target the real problem, reduce the stress and the stalker will disappear.

3. Historical/Survivor: Occasionally an adult who has been the victim of childhood incest will falsely report a rape. This is because they need to talk about a sexual issue in their life, but

can't yet disclose the incest. Decades of burying the truth and fearing that no one will believe them forces them to make up a story about a current sexual victimization. This opens the door for them to talk about their emotional problems surrounding sexual issues.

Again, when dealing with someone like this, you have to be careful not to "push them over the edge" and into suicide. Since you, *AS AN OFFICER*, are in a position of power, as was their father who molested them, you should not confront them with the "lie." It's much better to direct them to counseling so the real issues can be addressed.

This means that you'll have to take the rape report, which will waste a few hours of your time. However, an officer (usually male) doing and saying the right thing to someone like this is the ethical thing to do and is another example of *STRENGTH THROUGH ASSOCIATION*.

4. The Exhibitionist: A true female exhibitionist can drive a police department crazy. They will hang out at the cop-stop and "show it all" to everyone on the graveyard shift, which sometimes ends with disciplinary action being taken against the officers. The same woman will parade half naked in their living rooms with the drapes open for all to see. They will also make false rape reports. These reports will be in the form of "woman down" calls. The officer will arrive to find the nude victim lying unconscious on the floor, with no head trauma. She miraculously regains consciousness after all of swing swift and half the fire department has seen her naked, and reports that she was struck on the head, from behind, by an unknown assailant, who must have removed her clothing and raped her. If you come across one of these types of "victims," don't interview her alone!

Fortunately, most of the fictitious rape reports don't have an identifiable suspect attached to the allegation. Most of the time the victim will create a situation in which she will not or cannot identify the suspect and there will be no leads, witnesses or physical evidence that might lead to a suspect.

An example of this is the woman who reports that she was approached in broad daylight, at the busiest intersection in town and dragged off by a suspect, whom she did not get a good look at, and was raped. She cannot give a description of the assailant nor can any witnesses be found.

Another example would be the suspect who wore a ski mask (in the middle of summer) and gloves and while holding the victim down with both his hands, managed to put on a condom before he raped her. Have you ever tried to put on a condom while wearing gloves?

The use of condoms by rapists is now quite common. They are aware of DNA evidence (it's probably what sent them to prison the first time) and they are fearful of getting a STD during the rape. The suspect using a condom does not mean that the report is false.

It is also common to see a delay in reporting of the rape in these fictitious cases. This allows the victim time to have laundered any evidence items or clothing and for her memory of the suspect to fade. In the case of the victim being pregnant or catching a STD, it takes a few weeks for these symptoms to develop, resulting in the late report.

A very general rule of thumb is that if the rape report sounds like a TV movie, then it's probably fictitious. Since the general public has no idea as to how real rapists actually think and act, they tend to make up a story based on what they have seen on television.

I want to restate, as strongly as possible, that just because a victim reports a rape that has one or more of these elements in it, it does not automatically mean that the report is false. However, the investigating officer needs to be aware of this possibility and, when appropriate, explore this possibility. This is done by asking general inquiry questions or background question of the victim, such as:

"How long have you lived here?"

"Do you have a boyfriend or husband?"

"Have you broken up with a boyfriend or husband?"

"Has anything like this happened to you before?"

These are phrased as general inquiry or background, as opposed to accusatory questions . They will frequently solicit the type of information that is helpful in establishing if a report is false or not.

In a legitimate rape report, the victim will be able to give you associated details about the assault. These are the same kind of details that the child will be able to give about a molestation allegation.

Rape Reports: Making it "Better Than it is"

Sometimes, officers feel the need to make the victim's activity at the time of a crime sound better than it actually was. What *occurred* is *not your responsibility; your responsibility is simply to document what took place.* If a victim tells you that she was drunk or had been using drugs, or had multiple sex partners prior to the rape, you simply have to document that. Don't feel that you have an obligation to "clean up" the victim. If she was dancing seductively on the night club dance floor with the suspect a few minutes prior to him raping her in the parking lot, then say that. There is no need to cover it up or downplay it.

Report Narrative: Stranger Rape

On August 3, 1997, at 0230 hours, I met with victim #97-123 (referred to as "victim") at her apartment. She told me that she had been sexually assaulted by someone who had broken into her apartment. I initially obtained a suspect description and his last known direction of travel and broadcast that information to assisting officers, who set up a perimeter and conducted an area search for the suspect.

I noticed that the victim had a bruised right eye, as if she had been punched in the face, and that her nose was bleeding slightly. There was also some swelling to the right side of her face. She was initially treated at the scene by paramedics and then transported to Martin Luther Hospital in Anaheim for medical follow-up and for an ASAV exam. I made arrangements for Officer Brown and for CSI officers to stay at the apartment where the crime had taken place to collect physical evidence and to photograph the scene.

Once I re-contacted the victim at the hospital, I took her into the doctors' lounge so I could interview her prior to the actual medical exam taking place.

The victim told me that yesterday, as is her normal routine, she got up at 6:30 a.m., prepared herself for work, and then went to work where she has a clerical position at a large factory. She stayed at work until about 5:00 p.m., at which time she returned to her residence to change clothes.

At about 6:30 p.m., she left her home to meet with a friend, Mary Smith, at the shopping mall. At the mall, the victim and her friend had dinner and then they shopped for several hours. The victim indicated she left the mall at around 9:30 p.m. and drove home. On the way home, she stopped at the Mobil gas station, one-half mile from her residence, to obtain gas prior to actually returning to her apartment. When she drove into the complex itself, she entered through the security gate and then parked in her assigned carport. The victim does not recall anyone following her home at this time. She then locked her car and walked directly to her apartment. Once she entered the apartment, shortly after 10:00 p.m., she locked the dead bolt lock behind her.

She said that she then prepared herself for bed. She actually went to bed around 11:00 p.m. wearing a long nightshirt and panties. She told me that she left the ground floor sliding glass patio door open about six inches for ventilation when she went to bed.

The victim also told me that she was watching television, as she normally did when she went to bed, and she normally falls asleep with the television on.

She said that she was awakened at around 2:30 a.m. when she felt a hand across her face. This startled her and she tried to sit up in bed. When she did this, she was struck in the face several times by the suspect.

The victim said that the suspect then told her to be quiet, while he held a knife in his right hand in front of her face. At this point, she noted that the suspect had taken a bath towel from out of the bathroom and actually covered up the television screen with it. The television itself was still on, but the light coming from the TV screen was now not sufficient enough for her to get a good look at his face. The victim told me that she was fearful that the suspect might kill her if she did not comply with his demands.

He then took her by the arm and had her get out of bed. While holding the knife to her throat, he walked her through the apartment to ensure that no one else was there. During this time, he asked her if she lived alone and if she had a boyfriend. She replied that she does have a boyfriend, but that he does not live at that location, and there was no one else living in the apartment. While being taken through the apartment by the suspect, she saw that the sliding glass door was now standing wide open.

While the suspect was walking her through the apartment, he seemed very nervous and agitated. He talked to her in a very demeaning fashion and demanded to know the last time she had "fucked" her boyfriend.

The suspect then walked the victim back into the bedroom, at which time he ordered her to take her clothing off. Once she was nude, he told her to lie on her back on the bed. He continued to demand that she not look at him and that she keep her eyes closed.

The suspect then loosened his belt, unbuttoned his jeans, and dropped his pants down to his ankles. He was also wearing a button-up-the-front dress shirt that he did not remove or unbutton. The victim said that she saw that the suspect did not have an erection. He put the knife down on the night stand and then began to masturbate himself. The suspect still had difficulty in gaining an erection and, at this point, he became very agitated and called the victim a "bitch" and "whore." He then demanded that she begin to masturbate herself in front of him. Initially, the victim refused, but as the suspect approached her and said he would kill her if she did not comply, she began to fondle her vaginal area as directed by the suspect.

After doing this for perhaps a minute or two, the suspect was able to gain an erection. The suspect then attempted to have vaginal intercourse with the victim by lying on top of her; however, he was unable to maintain an erection and actual intercourse was not achieved at this time.

The suspect again became angry and agitated and demanded that the victim perform oral sex on him. She sat up on the edge of the bed and, with the suspect standing in front of her, he ordered that she put his penis into her mouth. She stated that she complied and performed oral sex on the suspect for perhaps a minute to a minute and a half.

During this time, the suspect began to stroke the victim's hair and stated, "I know you love it, baby, I know you love it." The victim indicated that the suspect then told her to lie back down on the bed. At this time, she saw that his demeanor had changed and that he was now less agitated than before and was acting somewhat robot-like in his actions and his demeanor with her. The suspect told the victim to lie back down on the bed, at which time he began to perform oral sex on her. The victim said that the suspect placed his mouth on her vagina for perhaps two to three minutes.

The suspect then lay on top of the victim and was successful in penetrating her vagina with his penis. She stated that they had intercourse for a short length of time, and then he got off from on top of her and stopped having intercourse with her. He then told her to roll over onto her stomach, at which time he then penetrated her vagina from the rear. The victim stated they had intercourse in this position for perhaps two to three more minutes. During this time, the suspect told her to repeat the phrase, "You're the best; you're the best I've ever had."

The suspect then withdrew his penis from her body and had the victim sit on the edge of the bed as he masturbated himself in front of her. He then ejaculated onto the carpeting adjacent to the bed itself.

The suspect then pulled his pants back up but did not allow the victim to dress herself. He then asked her where her jewelry box was, at which point she directed him toward the dresser on the opposite side of the bedroom. He then went to the dresser and took a 14 karat gold necklace with a small heart-shaped pendant on it from out of the jewelry box and placed it in his pocket.

The suspect then had the victim, who was still nude, walk from the bedroom area into the living room, where he had her sit on the sofa. The suspect then explained to the victim that his girlfriend was pregnant and had not had sex in several months. He was somewhat apologetic in his statements to her, but told her that he was always very careful to be sure not to hurt anyone when he had sex with them. He also demanded that the victim repeat the phrase, "It's okay. I wanted to have sex with you. You didn't hurt me." After repeating this phrase to the suspect several times, the suspect stated that he was going to leave. He also told her that she should not leave her sliding glass door open in the future. The suspect then left via the front door.

The victim stated that when the suspect left by the front door, he did not unlock the dead bolt lock in order to exit, indicating that he must have unlocked this door prior to making first contact with the victim.

The victim said that she did not hear or see a vehicle leaving the area after the suspect fled her apartment. The victim added that once the suspect was outside of the apartment, she went to the front door and closed and locked it to ensure that he would not return. The victim stated she then called her boyfriend, Jeff Jones, and told him that she had been raped. The boyfriend, who lives several miles away, told the victim to hang up the phone and call "911" in order to get the police to respond immediately to her home.

Dr. Smith performed the medical examination on the victim. He later told me that there was evidence of vaginal trauma that was consistent with the history given by the victim. The medical staff also treated the victim for her blackened eye and bloody nose, but stated that these injuries were superficial and not life-threatening. The doctor supplied me with the rape kit evidence that he had obtained during the examination of the victim, which I booked into evidence at the police department.

The hospital staff had called the county's Victim-Witness Office, who had a worker respond to the hospital. Also, the victim's sister was contacted and came to the hospital with some fresh clothing. The clothing that the victim wore to the hospital was taken for evidentiary purposes. After the medical exam was completed, the victim left the hospital with her sister and the Victim-Witness counselor.

I also relayed the information back to the officers at the victim's apartment as to the location of the possible evidence (seminal fluid) on the floor next to the bed and the information that a necklace had been taken from the jewelry box and that the suspect had prepared an exit prior to committing the actual rape.

The victim also indicated that the last time she had consensual intercourse was perhaps eight to ten days ago with her boyfriend.

Date Rape / Acquaintance Rape

Date rape suspects are sexual predators just as stranger rapists are, however, they have a slightly different method of operation. You can liken the difference between a date rape versus the stranger rape to a con man who commits a theft by fraud versus a bank robber who takes over a bank at gunpoint and steals money from the tellers. In the date rape scenario, the suspect is more like the con man who makes contact with the victim and then waits until the victim is particularly vulnerable, such as intoxicated, before he attempts a sexual assault.

Because of this acquaintance/prior relationship between the victim and suspect, these cases are more difficult to prosecute. It is quite possible that the victim has had prior consensual sex with the suspect or she has been in a relationship with the suspect that would tend to make people believe that the relationship has been sexual in nature. Quite often, the date rape scenario involves a situation where the victim has been drinking and/or using drugs and may have been doing this with the suspect.

Frequently, the sexual assault itself has the same dynamics as the stranger rape. The difference comes in the way the suspect approaches, contacts, and captures the victim. Once the capture is complete, the suspect may act out the same sort of rape fantasy that the stranger suspect has.

Because of the similarities, you interview the date rape victim in the same fashion as you would the victim of a stranger rape. You start with the first contact between her and the suspect and continue through the actual assault itself and the post-assault behavior.

Many of these date rape scenarios are not reported immediately. However, if the incident is reported within 72 hours of the actual sexual assault, you need to take the victim to the hospital for a sexual assault medical exam, just like any other sexual assault case. There is, however, an added difficulty in doing the ASAV exam in a date rape. The medical examination looks for abrasions, tearing, etc. consistent with a forced sexual penetration. Frequently, this evidence will not be present during a date rape scenario. This is because if the victim has been kissing or fondling the suspect prior to the actual rape, the female body will frequently prepare itself for intercourse. Then when the victim says, "no," but the suspect continues his advances, with the female body already prepared for intercourse, sometimes you will not find the vaginal trauma that you will find in a stranger rape.

Remember that you, the officer, are not responsible for the scenario that led up to the rape. If the victim was dancing naked in front of twenty people at a party and then states that one of them forced intercourse on her, then that is exactly how your report should read. Your job as an officer is to collect as much data as you can and then let the District Attorney and the court decide if it is a prosecutable case or not.

Report Narrative: Date / Acquaintance Rape

On Thursday, 12-11-97 at 1400 hours, I met with the victim, 97-138 (Betty) at her apartment along with her sister, witness Nelson. Betty told me that she wanted to report that she had been the victim of an acquaintance rape that had occurred on Sunday evening, 12-09-97.

Betty said she works for an insurance company in a middle management position. She told me that on Sunday, 12-07-97, it had been arranged for her and some of her coworkers to meet with some customers for a champagne brunch. This meeting was to be "half business and half pleasure." There were to be eight to ten people present at the brunch, and it was tentatively arranged that Betty was to meet the suspect in this case, who was a customer from the client company. Although there was no official "blind date" set up between Betty and the suspect, there was an understanding that if she and the suspect were to become acquainted during the champagne brunch, it might lead to a dating relationship. Betty indicated that she has been divorced for two years and currently does not have a boyfriend.

Betty said she and her friends met Sunday at about 11:00 a.m. at the restaurant and engaged in the meeting/social function. Betty said that she met the suspect and they seemed to get along quite well. The brunch lasted for several hours. Betty said at about 4:00 p.m., the brunch ended, and she decided to drive to the suspect's nearby apartment to leave her car at his apartment while they went somewhere else for the rest of the day. Betty stated that after having parked her car in the suspect's apartment complex, she got into his car and they drove to the beach, where they walked and talked for several more hours. Ultimately, they went to dinner together and then went dancing at a nightclub.

Betty stated that during the entire time she was with the suspect, he was very polite and cordial and that they did drink through the champagne brunch and at dinner and while dancing. She stated that although she was feeling the effects of the alcohol, she was not drunk. Betty also stated that while dancing, she did kiss the suspect on the lips while on the dance floor.

Betty said that around 10:30 p.m. they returned to the suspect's apartment. While still sitting in his car parked in the parking lot area, she had given him her telephone number and asked him to call her later on in the week. Betty then said that she needed to use the restroom prior to driving home. She went up to the suspect's apartment to use his bathroom.

Betty stated that upon entering the suspect's apartment, he directed her toward the master bathroom, which was actually located inside the master bedroom. After using the restroom, she came back out into the bedroom area and saw that the suspect was now standing in the doorway and blocking her exit from the bedroom, wearing only his boxer shorts. The suspect said something to the effect of "The evening's not over yet." Betty responded by telling him that she was not desirous of having any sort of sexual contact with him, and asked if he would step aside so she could leave the apartment.

Betty stated the suspect's demeanor had completely changed at this time. She stated he had been gentlemanly throughout the entire day and evening, but now he appeared to be very agitated and angry. She stated she tried to force her way past him in the doorway, but he simply grabbed her by the shoulders and pushed her back into the room. When she again stepped toward the doorway to try to exit, he punched her twice in the face using his left fist. Being punched in the face caused a great deal of pain and she sat down on the bed while holding her hands to her face. The suspect then approached her, pushed her down on the bed, and told her that she was going to "suck my dick."

Betty said she was fearful that the suspect might continue to hit her. She added that he is much larger than she, and was still in a very angry and agitated state. When he exposed his erect penis from the opening of his boxer shorts, she did, in fact, orally copulate him.

Betty stated that when the suspect told her to remove her clothing, she complied, adding that her left eye was starting to swell closed and she was fearful that she would be struck again. She removed all of her clothing and lay down on the bed as instructed. The suspect then performed oral sex on her vaginal area and then had vaginal intercourse with her. After completing the vaginal intercourse, the suspect told her that she was free to leave. He added that what had happened was only "rough sex" and that she should not be concerned about it. He also told her that he would call her later on in the week to make arrangements to see her again.

Betty said she dressed herself, left the apartment and drove home. Once at home, she called her sister, witness Nelson, and asked her to come to her apartment to assist her. When Nelson arrived, Betty explained to her what had happened. At this time, Betty was holding an ice pack to her left eye. Betty was reluctant to go to the hospital and/or make a police report at that time. However, Nelson did take photographs of her face and eye, just in case she decided to make a report later on. This film has not yet been developed, and

Betty said that she would make it available to detectives within the next day or two.

I noted there was still some discoloration to Betty's left eye. She had covered most of this discoloration with make-up. I asked her to remove the make-up from the eye so that the photographs could be taken of her injuries.

While the photographs were being taken, I spoke with witness Nelson. She told me that she had been called around midnight two nights before by her sister. The victim was upset and crying at the time and stated that something had happened to her, but she would not elaborate over the phone.

When Nelson arrived at Betty's apartment, she saw that her left eye was swollen closed and that she was crying. Betty then told her sister that she had met the suspect at a champagne brunch, had spent the day with him, but when she tried to leave his apartment, he had struck her in the face and forced to have sex with him. Betty did not elaborate as to any of the details of the sexual assault itself to Nelson. Nelson stated that she spent the rest of the night with her sister, during which time Betty continued to cry and tremble when she would recall what happened to her. Nelson attempted to get her sister to call a rape crisis hot line that night and/or the police department, but Betty was afraid to do so.

Betty said the clothing she was wearing that night had not been laundered yet and was still in her dirty clothes hamper. I had a Crime Scene Investigator collect those items for evidence purposes.

Spousal Rape

Spousal rape usually is seen in two forms. The first is the ongoing sexual abuse of the spouse during the course of the marriage; the other is when the husband and wife have separated and the estranged husband comes back and rapes his estranged wife. California Penal Code Section 262 outlines the elements of Spousal Rape. (See your individual state laws.)

Ongoing Spousal Abuse

In this situation, you will have the basic abusive environment where the suspect/husband is routinely physically and emotionally abusing his wife. As a part of this ongoing belittling and abuse of the female, it is not unusual for the husband to continually force sexual acts with her in a way that is meant to degrade and humiliate her. It is difficult to prosecute these types of cases because the victim, in essence, is consenting to the sexual acts. In these types of relationships, the sexual assault is just one more weapon in the husband's arsenal to hurt and humiliate his wife.

The officer has to be sure that he is not judgmental of the victim when she reports having been subjected to perhaps years of sexual acts with the suspect, none of which she consented to, but which she never objected to either.

A part of your interview process should include a little bit of background history as to how the husband and wife met and if their relationship was ever "normal" in the beginning, and about what time it changed into this abnormal abusive relationship. The victim will normally relate an ongoing series of sexual assaults by the suspect/husband. You want to document the last time this happened in some detail. Normally, the last time there was a sexual assault, it happened just prior to the victim finally leaving the household and going to a women's shelter for protection. Since this is the most recent sexual assault, you will be in a position to collect physical evidence just as you would in any other rape scenario.

Report Narrative: Ongoing Spousal Rape

On 8-12-97, at 1100 a.m., I met with victim 97-076 (Nancy) in the lobby of the police department. She was accompanied by a volunteer (Mary) from the Women's Transitional Living Center (WTLC). Mary told me that the victim, Nancy, had come to WTLC two nights ago after having been sexually assaulted by her husband. She stated that Nancy was now willing to make a police report about the sexual assault.

I took Nancy and Mary into a private interview room where I could speak with them. Nancy told me that she has been married to the suspect for eight and a half years. She told me that for the first five years of their relations, everything seemed normal. However, after the birth of their first child, the suspect seemed to change. She stated that he began to drink and became argumentative with her quite frequently. She said that occasionally, he would actually become physically assaultive, slapping her and sometimes kicking her. She said these physical assaults would occur perhaps once every four or five months.

Nancy stated that two months ago, she gave birth to their second child. She told me it was a difficult delivery and she has been under a doctor's care since the delivery. Because of this, she has not been able to return to work as soon as she did after the first pregnancy. She told me that not returning to work has caused some financial strain on the family, and because of this, the suspect has become more argumentative with her and become more physically abusive.

Nancy told me it had not been unusual during the last several years of their relationship for the suspect to want to end an argument by having sex with her. She told me that normally, after he had been very angry and enraged, he would tell her that he wanted to show her that "he loved her," and even though they were arguing, he would demand that she have intercourse with him. She told me that she would comply with his requests for sex because she knew that after having sex with him, he was not likely to continue the physical assault.

Nancy said that three days ago, in the morning hours, her husband decided not to go to work, stating that he was not feeling well. At about 9:00 a.m., Nancy had finished feeding their infant and put him down for a nap. After doing so, the suspect approached her and demanded that they have intercourse, stating that "it's been long enough" and added that he felt her internal injuries had healed sufficiently for them to have sex. Nancy tried to explain to her husband that she still had some sporadic vaginal bleeding from internal injuries and she did not think it would be safe to have sex at that time. This agitated the suspect, who slapped her once across the face, stating that he wanted to have intercourse with her.

Nancy stated that she complied with his request and disrobed and lay down on top of the bed. She stated that he had intercourse with her for a couple of minutes until she started to bleed. The bleeding angered the suspect even more and he slapped her twice more across the face.

The suspect then demanded that she take a shower with him. They got into the shower in the master bathroom and he began to wash her body. Nancy stated she was confused by the suspect's actions because it was not normal for him to show any sort of concern for her, nor do they normally bathe together.

During the bathing process, however, the suspect took a bar of soap and inserted it into her vaginal canal telling her he thought this would cleanse her body. The bar of soap became lodged inside her vaginal cavity and he was unable to retrieve it. Later that day, Nancy had to go to her doctor to have the soap removed from her vagina.

Barbara stated that later that evening she decided to leave her husband and took both children and went to the WTLC where she has been housed since that time. (Note: To protect spousal abuse victims and prevent their whereabouts being determined by the abuser, the locations of all shelters are secret.) Barbara indicated that she could be reached through her sister, as indicated on the face sheet of the police report. (See Advocacy section for additional information on shelters.)

I then called Dr. Smith who confirmed that the victim had come to him for removal of the soap from her vagina.

Estranged Husband

It is not unusual to see an estranged husband and wife be involved in a sexual assault situation. Because of the emotional turmoil involved in a separation or divorce situation, often the male becomes very angry and needs to act out his anger in some fashion. He sees the ex-wife as being the source of all of his bad feelings and emotions.

Men have the ability to take all of their emotions, be they helplessness, sadness, anxiety, and turn them all into anger and then project the anger toward what they perceive to be source of all of these feelings. They want to feel better (balance the emotional teeter-totter in their head) by making the victim feel worse than they do. Through this projection of their feelings into the victim, they will often come back to the family home and sexually assault the victim.

In these scenarios, you have the same sort of rape dynamics as in any other sexual assault. You have an approach of the suspect toward the victim; there is the initial contact, which might be under the guise of wanting to reconcile the relationship, or making some sort of support payments. Then you have the capture part of the assault, where the ex-husband actually captures her just like in a stranger rape scenario.

You then have the assault itself, followed by the post-assault behaviors in which the husband will often blame the victim for what took place. In this type of scenario, the husband frequently sees the wife as being his personal property that he can possess and use in any way that he sees fit, including the forced sexual act.

In this type of scenario, you document the sexual assault just like you would any other assault and interview the victim accordingly.

Report Narrative: Estranged Husband Spousal Rape

On 2-6-98, I met with victim #98-36 (Jane) at the front desk of the police department. She stated that five days ago she had been raped by her estranged husband. I took her into an interview room to speak to her about the assault.

Jane said that she married the suspect four years ago. Within the last year, their relationship had deteriorated, and they had separated. Jane moved into an apartment by herself, which is where the crime occurred.

She said that Sunday afternoon, February 1st, she was lying by the swimming pool of her apartment complex when the suspect approached her on foot. The suspect told her that he wanted to talk about the divorce and the division of property. He said that he wanted to go into her apartment to discuss these matters.

Jane was fearful of him because it appeared that he had been drinking. She initially refused to go inside with him, but he told her that if she did not go inside with him, he would send copies of nude photographs of her to her family and friends. Jane told me that during their marriage the suspect had taken many sexually explicit photographs of her, some of them while posing with marital aids.

Jane said she was very interested in having these photos returned to her, so she agreed to go to the apartment with the suspect. Once inside, they began to argue and she asked the suspect to leave. She told him that she had to meet with some friends and needed to change clothes. She did this hoping that the suspect would leave so she could change. She entered her bedroom and removed her swimming suit at which time the suspect walked into the bedroom. They continued to argue while she was dressing. While Jane was still partially nude, the suspect demanded to know if she had a boyfriend or if she had been sexually active with anyone else. Jane told him that she had not been sexually active, but he did not believe her.

When she turned her back on him to step toward the closet, he grabbed her by the shoulders and threw her onto the bed. He then told her that she belonged to him. He then pulled the underwear off her lower body while sitting across her legs. She told me that she was afraid that he would hurt her by punching her in the face as he had two years prior when they had argued and he had been drinking.

The suspect took his pants off and she saw that he had an erection. He demanded that she have sex with him. He got on top of her and had intercourse for about three minutes. Jane said that she did not struggle with him at this time because she just wanted to get it over with, hoping he would not harm her. Prior to leaving the apartment, the suspect told her that if she reported the rape no one would believe her and he would deny it.

Jane stated she had since laundered the clothing and the bedding upon which the rape occurred. She delayed reporting the crime because she did not think anyone would believe her and she was still hopeful that the suspect would return the nude photos of her. She told me that last night she received a call from her mother telling her that the suspect had mailed several of these photographs to the mother and other family members. She decided to come to the police department to report the rape.

A rape examination was not done because of the time lapse between the rape and today's date.

Senile / Elderly Victims

This section is intended as a discussion about victims who are in retirement homes, nursing homes, or other types of care facilities. Because of their age, their medical problems and disabilities, they are very vulnerable to sexual assault. Also, as discussed earlier, they are seen as non-sexual, or asexual victims and are perfect targets for the type of offender that wants to assault this type of victim. Some sex offenders seek jobs as a night nurse or medical aid in a nursing home facility where they have access to countless numbers of victims who are perhaps nonverbal, or unable to report or resist any sort of sexual assault.

You, as a responding officer, need to obtain a lot of medical background from the doctors or nursing staff and the victim's family as a part of your investigation. You will have to understand exactly what types of physical and mental problems the victim has. This will give you an idea as to how she is able to relate what took place to you.

There is also the problem with the generation difference between you and the victim. You, as an officer, might have difficulty talking to someone who is older than your grandmother about a sexual issue. Also, the victim may have difficulty discussing the forced sexual act, as she came from a different time when such issues were not discussed at all. You may also have to identify body parts to be sure you and the victim are talking about the same thing. Since our language has grown and changed over the last several decades, you want to be sure that you and the victim are talking the same language when she talks about being forced into some sort of sexual act.

Because of vision problems, hearing problems, and all of the medical problems that accompany the aging process, the victim may not be able to identify the suspect in the usual fashion, such as showing her a photo lineup or even doing an in-person lineup.

Sometimes, this identification process is overcome by a witness who actually walked in on the assault as it was taking place. More often, it is accomplished by narrowing down the potential suspect pool circumstantially. You would do this by having one of the nurses who routinely checks on the victim, say on an hourly basis, indicate that the victim was clothed and was fine at midnight, but when she returned at 1:00 a.m., she found the victim to be upset, partially nude and bleeding. You then determine who had access to that victim, or who entered the room during that one-hour time frame, which would narrow down the possible suspect pool. Then the collection of physical evidence would become very important as far as using biological evidence, hairs and fibers to further identify the suspect.

Keeping all of this in mind, the actual interview of the victim should follow as closely as possible the interviewing techniques used for other sexual assault victims.

Report Narrative: Senile / Elderly Victim

On Saturday, 3-7-98, at 8:00 a.m., I received a radio call to respond to the Happy Hills Convalescent Hospital regarding a possible elder abuse and sexual battery. I spoke with Nurse Wilson who stated that she believed that one of the residents of the home had been assaulted. Wilson stated that at 3:00 a.m. this morning, she made her usual rounds and found that the victim was asleep and in good condition. At 7:00 a.m. while making her rounds, she observed a long cut across the victim's forehead and saw that her nightgown had been pulled to the side exposing her breasts. The victim told Wilson "he violated me."

Wilson stated that the victim is 89 years old and suffers from multiple medical problems, including a loss of eyesight and hearing and suffers from short-term memory loss, along with a heart condition and other ailments for which she takes medications. Her primary physician is Dr. Ross, who is out of town and won't be back until Monday.

Paramedics were called to the scene to examine the cut. They stated it was severe enough to require transportation to the emergency room for the victim to be treated. Prior to going to the emergency room myself, I had the convalescent home's staff roll up the bedding and place it into a paper bag for me to take as evidence. I also requested that the staff prepare a list of all employees that were on duty between midnight and seven.

When I arrived at the emergency room, Dr. Davis had closed the head wound with ten stitches and told me that the cut was not made by a sharp object such as a knife but was more likely caused by her being struck in the head and cut with a ring on someone's finger. Dr. Davis also conducted a vaginal examination of the victim due to the possibility of her having been raped. He told me that her vaginal opening was quite small and would require the use of a pediatric vaginal speculum to do the exam.

I made arrangements for the victim to be transported by private ambulance to Martin Luther Hospital where the staff is more experienced in conducting sexual assault exams. I attempted to interview the victim, but due to her age and her mental state (senility), all she would say was, "he violated me." I was of the opinion that this meant that she had been raped.

At Martin Luther Hospital, Dr. Adams conducted an ASAV exam on the victim. He told me that the victim's bladder had actually fallen into the vaginal canal which is not unusual for a woman her age. Once he lifted the bladder, he found that she had a normal vaginal opening and saw multiple tears and abrasions that were consistent with her having been raped. He also collected what he believed to be seminal fluid from the back of the vaginal vault. I obtained the sexual assault kit from the doctor for evidence.

Since the victim has no relatives living in the area, the private ambulance returned the victim to the convalescent home. I also returned and obtained the list of employees and the guest/visitor's sign-in book that is normally kept at the front desk. Anyone visiting the facility is required to sign in prior to visiting any resident.

Prior to leaving the facility I called the Elder Abuse Registry and asked them to arrange for alternative living arrangements for the victim.

Conditional Exam / Interview

The law allows, under certain circumstances, for the victim of a crime to be interviewed outside of the courtroom and then that interview be used for courtroom purposes. The law requires the defense counsel be present during this interview and that the defense have an opportunity to cross-examine the victim. As long as these requirements are met, the interview of the victim outside of the courtroom can be introduced later on as evidence in the trial itself.

When dealing with the extremely elderly victims, it is often necessary to conduct such a conditional exam in order to obtain their statements in case they die prior to trial. The conditional exam is generally set up between the assigned detective and the District Attorney's Office. A judge, court reporter, defense attorney, and even the defendant will be brought to the victim's hospital room so that the questioning can take place at the time. The law requires that the conditional exam be conducted with the suspect's lawyer present. If the suspect has not been arrested yet, or even identified yet, then you cannot conduct the exam.

In this situation, you might consider videotaping your interview with the victim in the hopes that the District Attorney could argue later in court that since the victim has now passed away, your videotaped interview might be used in lieu of her testimony. I don't know of any court decision at this time that will allow that, but it at least would be one way of preserving the victim's testimony on the chance that she might die prior to going to court.

When you have a suspect who is operating inside a nursing home, you may have multiple victims. Since many of the victims will be aged or in ill health, and the possibility exists that they may not live long enough for the case to make it to court, the videotape may be your one hope of presenting corroborative evidence as to MO, as in a signature-type crime, or for sentencing or other legal issues.

Elderly victims are very vulnerable to sexual assault. To successfully prosecute these extremely difficult cases, the responding officer has to do a very thorough and in-depth investigation.

Mentally Handicapped / Retarded Victims

There is an entirely different set of issues you may run into when dealing with an adult who has some severe mental disabilities or retardation. These people grow up in an entirely different environment than the rest of society and, as a result, their culture is actually different than yours or mine. They have grown up in a culture where they have been taught to be compliant. Also, their lives are very structured. They have people who help them get up in the morning, help them clean themselves, bathe themselves, dress themselves, help them eat, take them to their daily activities, feed them lunch, help them in their afternoon activities, and then bring them back to their residence where they again help them clean, bathe, and prepare for bed. Almost every minute of the day is scheduled for them. Their entire schooling/training has been to get them to accept the routine and to do the routine as best as their abilities allow them to do. Because of this, they have been rewarded for being compliant and for doing whatever their caretakers require them to do.

This "learned compliance" makes them very vulnerable victims. Depending on which study you want to review, handicapped adults are victimized at a rate of two to ten times more frequently than non-handicapped adults.

Background Information

Prior to approaching an interview with such a person, you need to obtain as much medical background about them as possible. If you can, locate their primary care provider and ask this person what you can expect from the victim as far as language levels and their ability to interact with you. This will give you a great deal of insight as to how to approach the victim. If you can have this primary care provider assist you in the interview of the victim, that would be of great benefit.

Don't assume that because the victim has an IQ or the "mental age" of a five-year-old, that the victim wants to be talked to as you would talk to a five-year-old. Depending on the victim's life experiences, they may have some abilities similar to an adult and they would generally prefer to be talked to on that level. This is the type of information you can obtain from the primary care provider.

Interview: Mentally Handicapped / Retarded Victim

When talking to this type of victim, you want to be sure you maintain a comfortable distance from them physically. This is a distance that makes the victim comfortable talking to you. Unlike dealing with a small child, where you want to sit close to them so you can interact with them and touch them, you want to do just the opposite with someone in this category. It is quite possible that the person will object to being touched or having you too close to them and they might violently react to any such invasion of their "space."

It may take several separate contacts with the victim until they feel comfortable enough to talk to you at all, let alone talk about the sexual assault. Once you do establish a rapport with them, you have to be sure you are speaking the same language. Identifying body parts and terminology is very important. Most of these people have been taught human anatomy and have proper names for their body parts. This has been done for hygiene reasons and to teach them about sexuality, in general. It is not unusual for someone who you might consider to be retarded to use proper body names for their genitals.

The severely handicapped/retarded have many care providers in contact with them throughout the week. As a result, the list of potential suspects could be quite lengthy.

Interviewing someone with a physical or mental handicap requires a lot of patience on the part of the officer. There are variations within the abilities that each of these people have, so don't assume that because someone is retarded that they can't give you an accurate description of what took place. The difficulty comes in being able to understand their speech, and being sure that you are speaking the same language they are. The primary care provider for such a person should be consulted during the course of the interview to be sure that you are understanding what the victim is saying.

If you come into a care facility where one patient is pregnant, you should suggest to the staff of the nursing home that they check the other female patients for pregnancy and sexually transmitted diseases.

Report Narrative: Mentally Handicapped / Retarded Victim Report

On 9-15-97 at 1515 hours, I met with the reporting party, Natalie Johnson, at Canyon Valley High School. Canyon has a student body population that includes students that are in Special Education or have special needs, such as being handicapped or retarded. Mrs. Johnson works within that part of the campus that deals with these special needs children.

Mrs. Johnson told me she was concerned about victim 97-1101 (Alice). Alice is a seventeen-year-old female who has a mental capability of a six-to-seven-year-old. Mrs. Johnson said that earlier today, Alice began to complain that her stepfather was fondling her breasts and making her feel uncomfortable every time she was with him. Mrs. Johnson added that Alice lives in a residential care facility during the week which transports her to Canyon Valley High School each day for her daily activities. On weekends, she returns home to live with her biological mother and stepfather.

Mrs. Johnson stated that Alice is a rather passive teenager who is often shy around strangers. She suggested that I not attempt to get too close to Alice for fear that she might run away. She also stated that when Alice starts to like somebody, it is not unusual for her to grab them in a "bear hug" and not let go for several minutes. Because of this behavior, Mrs. Johnson suggested that during my initial contacts with her, I sit across the desk from her in order to not invade her "space." Mrs. Johnson added that Alice has a rather complete vocabulary, but she speaks with a lisp and also drools when speaking. This makes it rather difficult to understand her at times. She suggested that I speak very slowly to Alice and then listen very carefully to what she was saying. Although Alice has some mental deficits, she can understand simple questions and can carry on a normal conversation.

Alice was brought into Mrs. Johnson's office and Mrs. Johnson was present during the interview. I was introduced to Alice and sat at a table with her. In order to establish a rapport with Alice, I began to draw a stick figure of a female on some notebook paper I had. I then asked Alice if she wanted to help me complete the drawing and she then drew some clothing onto the stick figure. Since Mrs. Johnson told me that Alice had been taught the proper names for both male and female anatomy, I did not see a need to identify body parts during this initial process. However, this developed a rapport between

Alice and me, which allowed me to begin to ask if anything "bad" ever happened to her when she returned home on weekends.

Alice told me that sometimes her stepfather makes her walk around the house without her "top" on. She also stated there were times when he had actually come up behind her and placed his arms around her, putting his hands on both of her breasts when she was not wearing clothes. She told me that this happened both in the bathroom and the bedroom.

I asked Alice if she could remember what happened during the first incident . She said that her stepfather had initially started by rubbing her back, which made her feel good. She went on to state that after rubbing her back, he reached around and initially squeezed her breasts over her clothing. She said that after that, he would begin to squeeze her breasts both over and under her clothing. Alice was unable to give any sort of time frame as to when this first started to happen, nor could she give me an idea as to the number of times it occurred.

Alice said that these touching incidents made her "feel sad." She also added that she was afraid to tell her mother about what was happening because she knows that her mother loves the suspect.

Nothing further was gained from the interview with Alice.

Mrs. Johnson stated she was going to contact Alice's social worker and make arrangements to be sure that Alice was safe the next time she returned home for the weekend.

Satanic Cults

The mere existence of Satanic cults is of no interest to law enforcement unless they are involved in illegal activities. The only time they are of interest to the sex crime investigator is when individuals allege they have been sexually victimized as part of cult activities or the cult is using minors for sexual purposes during their activities. There have also been claims that cult members have been "baby breeders" and that these babies were conceived specifically for the purpose of being sacrificed during satanic activities.

Obviously, reports of mass homicides of infants by any organized group are very serious accusations. Many such crimes have been investigated by agencies, including the FBI, and to my knowledge, none of the claims were able to be proven. Occasionally, you will encounter a victim who claims to have either witnessed such satanic homicides or have been the victim of some sort of sexual assault by one or more members of the cult.

Interviewing someone who claims to be a victim of a crime resulting from ritual activity is relatively easy. From my experience, the best way to interview someone like this is simply to allow them to tell their story. These individuals are more than willing to tell their story to *anyone* who will listen. Many of them have ended up on the television talk show circuit, explaining about their victimization and the crimes they had witnessed.

Once they have finished telling you their story, you can ask them about specific details of the events that, if they actually occurred, would be easy to recall. There are key areas upon which to focus when asking about the specific details.

You first want to *ask about the location where the satanic acts took place.* Some of the more common responses will be motel rooms, churches that are closed for renovation, and remote, outdoor locations in the open desert or mountains. Usually, you will be given very vague recollections of the locations themselves.

With regard to motel rooms, often the victim will describe a room that is, in actuality, too small for all of the described activity to have occurred. When it comes to renovated churches, very rarely can the victims actually identify the location. The same holds true for outdoor locations; they cannot find them. It has been my experience that these types of victims cannot direct you back to the scene of the cult activity that holds any evidence that such an event took place.

Ask the victim *whether or not they suffer from Multiple Personality Disorder and, if so, what type of treatment or medication are they taking.* Frequently, you will find that they are in a group therapy situation, hearing similar stories from other members of the support group and the victim's statements would possibly be considered cross-contaminated.

A common theory regarding the lack of identifiable suspects and locations is that within one of the personalities, the entire cult and related activity exists and is acted out, as opposed to actually occurring "outside," in reality. We can neither support this theory or refute that statement since an in-depth discussion of Multiple Personality Disorder is not germane to this text.

Another key question for the reporting party is *to name the identities and occupations of the other members of the cult.* Typically, you will be told that some are law enforcement personnel, members of the clergy and sometimes a local mortician. These professional members serve several purposes. Believing some police officers are cult members, victims have been reluctant to come forward to law enforcement for fear that they would be speaking to another cult member and that any investigation could be derailed by members of the cult who are also law enforcement officers. According to the victim, the clergy members supply the locations for the satanic activities to take place as well as use their position in churches to recruit additional cult members. According to the reporting party, the local mortician has the responsibility of disposing of the bodies that have been sacrificed during the satanic gathering.

While questioning the victim about associated details concerning the event, try to focus in on the mortician angle. Most people have very limited knowledge about morticians, so their descriptions of a mortician's activities will be very vague at best. Some of the more common descriptions of the mortician's participation is that he brings a portable crematorium to the satanic activity location and after "the babies are murdered," they are disposed of in the portable crematorium. You should ask for as detailed a description as possible of this portable crematorium. You may also want to ask how the local mortician has the portable crematorium registered with the Department of Motor Vehicles. Is it (a) a recreational vehicle, (b) a sport utility vehicle, (c) a commercial vehicle, or (d) none of the above since there is no such thing.

The amount of heat necessary to cremate the human body is tremendous. To my knowledge, there is no way to adequately insulate any sort of portable/mobile vehicle that could actually sustain such heat. Once the body is cremated, the bones have to be pulverized in order to properly dispose of them. Is the vehicle a combination incinerator and crusher? I think not.

Inquire of the victim if she believes she has been programmed by members of the cult. I have been told that victims were programmed to participate in the satanic activities by way of a post-hypnotic suggestion and other mind controlling methods used by cults. One 38 -year-old victim told me that as a child, cult members had used the touch tone phone sounds to preprogram her. Now, as an adult, when she heard these tones on her phone, she would go into a "zombie-like" state, then leave her home and join the cult for the evening's activity, leaving with no memory of what had transpired due to a post-hypnotic suggestion. The problem with her revelation however, was that when this childhood programming (using the touch tone phone to trigger her behavior) supposedly took place, it would have happened at a time when touch tones had not yet been introduced.

Usually a recounting of the crime and behavior will contain a statement from the reporting party about being controlled by "supernatural powers." According to what I have been told, cult members use some form of mental telepathy to force the victim to go to a location, participate in satanic rituals (that normally include unwanted sexual activity between the victim and cult members), as well as occasionally causing the victim to levitate. Some have reported that the mind control is strong enough to block the victim's memory as to where and what events took place during the cult activity.

One of the last things you should solicit from the victim is past addresses. This will allow background information to be obtained to see if there have been similar reports made by that victim in other cities. Since many of these victims are tenacious in their reports to law enforcement, wanting something done about a crime they truly believe happened, it is necessary to document their statements as thoroughly as possible.

The steps toward proving or disproving an allegation of cult rape are exactly the same as in any other rape complaint. The purpose of your investigation, in this case, is *not* to disprove the statements made by the victim; you are asking questions designed to solicit the truth. Once the truth is discovered, it will automatically point toward a legitimate crime, or a fictitious one.

Unlawful Intercourse

California law has been changed so as to be "gender neutral." As a result, anyone, male or female, who has sexual intercourse with someone under the age of 18, be they male or female, is in violation of the law.

Generally speaking, these cases involve an underage female having sex with an older boyfriend. Frequently, the girl's parents find out about this by reading her diary or they discover that the daughter is pregnant, and they want to press criminal charges against the boyfriend. The parents are not allowed by law to press charges against anybody. Pressing charges is something that the District Attorney's Office does. Also, since hearsay in this issue is not admissible, the reading of the child's diary, or any spontaneous statements made by the child, do not constitute the elements of a crime.

In this type of situation, you need the victim to actually come forward and talk about having sexual intercourse with her boyfriend, that it occurred within your county, and that it occurred within the statute of limitations.

If you have a victim who is willing to do this, the interview process with her is very simple. All you have to do is establish a general time frame as to when the intercourse took place, that it was consensual in nature, that it was actual vaginal intercourse, *and* that the suspect knew that she was under age. The age issue is normally satisfied by the victim having told the suspect how old she is, by his having picked her up at a junior high school on several occasions, or by his attending her 15th birthday party, or by some other such means.

There is no reason to go into any great detail as to the actual sexual acts themselves. If the minor can indicate she was having vaginal intercourse with the suspect twice a week, every week for the past two months, and that it occurred at his house after school, then that is normally sufficient to fulfill the elements of a crime.

In these types of cases, it is also very easy to get the suspect to confess to having intercourse with the girl. Normally, if they are in a boyfriend-girlfriend relationship, he will be somewhat reluctant at first, but ultimately he will admit to being involved in that relationship and that it got "carried away" to where they were having intercourse, but that it was consensual in nature. Once you have those elements identified, that's really all you need to prosecute the suspect criminally.

Report Narrative: Unlawful Intercourse

On 9-1-97 at 1600 hours, I met the victim's mother at her residence. The mother said that she had read the victim's diary and learned that she had been involved in a sexual relationship with her 25-year-old-boyfriend. The victim is fourteen years of age.

I interviewed the victim, who told me that about four months ago, she was introduced to the suspect via mutual friends. They struck up a friendship and, ultimately, a dating relationship.

The victim said that for the last two months, every Friday after school, she has been picked up at school by the suspect. They would then drive to his home since his parents were not at home on Friday afternoons. The victim told me that they would engage in consensual vaginal intercourse, usually twice each afternoon, at the suspect's home, in his bedroom. The victim stated that during these acts of consensual intercourse, she never used any sort of birth control or "protection." She added that she feels she might be pregnant at this time, as she is three weeks overdue in having her period. She added that she has told the suspect that she might be pregnant, and he indicated that he wants to help her raise the baby if she is, in fact, pregnant.

I telephoned the suspect from the victim's home. He identified himself by full name, birth date, address, and driver's license number. At first, he was reluctant to talk about his sexual relationship with the victim. However, I told him that the victim was possibly pregnant, and genetic testing of the infant would identify that he was the father. He then told me that he had, in fact, been involved in a consensual sexual relationship with the victim.

The suspect said that every Friday afternoon, for the last couple of months, he would pick the victim up at school, drive her to his home where they would engage in consensual intercourse in his bedroom. He added that he knew the victim was underage, but felt that it was okay to have sex with her because they were in love with each other.

To Tape or Not to Tape

Throughout this text, I have talked about the pros and cons of taping conversations. It may seem from the generalities made in this handbook that I am totally against tape-recording interviews; this is not the case. I am against routinely tape-recording conversations without having any understanding as to why it's being done. As I have said many times, the law does not require law enforcement to tape record anybody. Obviously, there are many instances when tape- recording someone is of great value. Suspect interviews would be one of these exceptions, as would reluctant witnesses or anyone who you think would change their story at a later date. Also, if you get that "gut feeling," or instinct that you need to tape-record somebody, then by all means, do so.

There have been times when I have been in court and questioned by the defense attorney as to why I did not tape-record a victim or a witness. The response to that question is, "There are several reasons why I did not." If the attorney inquires further as to what those reasons are, the answer should be:

1. "First of all, there is nothing in law that requires me to tape record anybody."

2. "I really did not have the ability to tape-record that particular witness at that time."

3. "I know that the rule of court is that any interviews that are tape-recorded have to be transcribed in order to be introduced into evidence, and transcribing an interview is a very

time-consuming and costly process. It is the informal policy of my agency and me to not routinely tape-record people because transcribing those tapes is very labor intensive."

4. "It is my personal policy to only tape-record those individuals who I think might change their stories at a later date. My experience has been that suspects routinely do this, especially after they have talked with their defense lawyer, who may have suggested that they come up with a different version as to what actually transpired. Also, there are situations where family members might change their story for one reason or another, or in drug-related crimes such as homicide, where this type of witness routinely changes his story because of the subculture in which they live.

5. "I also might decide to tape-record someone if I had a *gut feeling* that there was a need to do that for some reason. In this particular case, since none of these elements existed, I decided not to tape-record my interview with the victim."

When the Victim Won't Talk

It would be irresponsible of us to not tell you of those situations where, in spite of glaring evidence, a victim will not disclose to you, or will adamantly deny that anything took place. This has happened on numerous occasions, and in spite of eyewitness accounts, we have had victims who will not, for whatever reasons, tell you what happened to them.

We believe it is far better to accept that reluctance at the first contact rather than have five interviews where the victim says "nothing happened," then on the sixth, because of trust building or finally being tired of the victimization, they decide to tell you of their plight. You can be assured that a defense attorney can create a great deal of "reasonable doubt" about the validity of this victim's testimony by calling into evidence the first five interviews where they denied the crime.

As harsh as it sounds, our advice is to simply walk away, close the file, and go on to a victim who wants help. Protect the ones you can—the ones who are ready to be protected. The rest, unfortunately, may stay victims. Taking this approach always leaves the door open for a victim who may, at some future point, determine that they want to do something about the crime committed against them. Opening files is much easier than facing an experienced defense attorney with countless "nothing happened" interview reports that exonerate his client or would at least establish doubt.

While we may receive some criticism for this "walk away if they won't talk" position, we feel it is in the best interest of the victim to do so. We would rather take the knocks than see the victims experience them in court!

Female Anatomy

Over the last several years, there has been an increase in the technology used in the performance of the actual pelvic exam of a rape victim. Specifically, the use of a colposcope to help in the examination that leads to a lot more physical findings of force and trauma than was ever found in the past. Also, there are now nurse practitioners and doctors who specialize in this type of examination, who actually know what to look for and, as a result, the physical findings are more dramatic than they have been in the past.

During consensual intercourse, the female body goes through several anatomic changes in order to allow for vaginal penetration and then to trap the seminal fluid in the back of the vaginal vault in order to assist in conception. In a non-consenting act of intercourse, this body preparation does not take place. An experienced medical practitioner can find blunt force type of trauma and irritation/friction type injuries to the inside of the vaginal canal. Tearing to the posterior fourchette, and even bruising to the cervix itself, is not unusual evidence to be found during a properly conducted medical examination. The tissues inside the vagina are similar in consistency to the inside of a mouth or a cheek. These tissues are easily damaged during the forced sexual assault. They also heal quickly.

With the aid of the colposcope, which is basically an optical viewing device used to look inside the vaginal vault, the doctor can actually see the small, microscopic tearing inside the vaginal area that is consistent with forced intercourse. With the aid of a purple dye (toluidine blue) which adheres to the cell membranes that have been damaged by the friction of the intercourse, it is also quite easy to see that the vaginal area has, in fact, been damaged by this nonconsensual sex.

The colposcope has the ability to photograph the internal injuries that the female has received. Quite often, these internal injuries are the only physical evidence you will find to support the victim's statement about a nonconsensual sexual act.

The study of human sexual response as it relates to vaginal trauma is ongoing. When completed, this data should assist in the interpreting of ASAV examinations.

Teaming Officers and Advocates

The officer and the advocate have two very different roles, both designed to accomplish the same end; prosecution of the suspect and restoring the victim to a healthy life.

The advocate as used in this text is *not* the social worker or child protective services worker who might accompany the officer at the time of the initial interview. The advocate is a person from the county victim witness program, or the volunteer from CASA (Court Appointed Special Advocates), or the local nonprofit agency individual that is willing to help.

The advocate usually enters the case *after* the initial interview. Depending on their agency's protocol, they may be limited to entering the case only after it has been filed with the District Attorney's office. In situations involving rape, they will come out twenty fours a day, seven days a week, upon request from the police, usually meeting the officer at the hospital at the time that the sexual assault exam is being done.

The nonprofit organization advocate will enter whenever requested to do so, whether the case has been filed or not. Sometimes, they are the originator of the information that leads to a case. Since advocates from nonprofit agencies are *not* tied to county protocols, they have more latitude in what they can or will do.

The officer and the advocate must always keep in mind that the advocate is there to assist, *not take over the police investigation, collect evidence or do the interview.* Initially, the advocate should be given an outline of the case at hand, which would contain all of the necessary information they need to be effective. After that, any investigative information, new allegations, facts, incidents, or other information should flow from the advocate *to the officer.* It is important that the victim knows that the advocate is providing this new information to the officer in order to strengthen the case. This way the victim does not feel betrayed by the advocate.

Avoiding full disclosure of all details of the case to the advocate preserves the integrity of the case and prevents the advocate from being put in an awkward situation in the future. Never put the advocate in a position where they know more about the case than they should. This might place them under suspicion if there is a leak to the victim, suspect or press.

REMEMBER—THE OBJECTIVE OF ANY INTERVIEW IS TO GAIN INFORMATION, NOT GIVE IT OUT!! In addition to providing information to an officer, the advocate's job is to assist with the victim's psychological needs and to explain general procedures and protocols. With that in mind, the advocate does not need, nor usually want, all of the microscopic details that simply muddy their relationship with the victim.

THIS PAGE INTENTIONALLY LEFT BLANK

SECTION 2
THE ADVOCATE

THIS PAGE INTENTIONALLY LEFT BLANK

CHAPTER 6

THE ADVOCATE'S PERSPECTIVE

While Detective Howell has given you excellent tools for interviewing children and adults and presenting a case for prosecution, he didn't tell you that one of the reasons he is so effective in his work is that he genuinely cares about the victims. A basic ingredient for every individual who is pursuing a career where they will be working with victims is that they must be caring and compassionate in addition to being effective.

As an advocate for children, I have been fortunate to work with thousands of victims and several hundred law enforcement officers. Cases have ranged from emotional abuse to the kidnapping and murder of a child. I *know* what victims need—I have walked in their shoes, both as a child and an adult. The alliances I have formed with law enforcement officers, like Detective Howell, have allowed me to maximize the services available to the victims and their families and minimize the trauma of the victimization.

My intent is to give you food for thought—basic insights into things that have lost cases, allowed a child to slip through the cracks in the system, and for a few, tragically, cost them their lives. Each of the incidents and case studies are set out not to mock or criticize the officers or professionals who did it wrong—it is to help you avoid making the same mistakes.

Detective Howell has told you to: *Get it all, Get it right, Get it the first time.* A simple policy to remember, but I'm asking you to add a fourth "basic" which is to *"Think about it"*. Think about the simple things that can change the destiny of a case—and an individual.

Child Victims: "Potholes in the Road that Leads to Justice"

When you are to interview a child who has been victimized *within* their own family, do it *spontaneously* at the school or at home. Too often, some law enforcement agencies and social service agencies, will phone to set up an appointment at a future date and time to interview a child. Not only does that place the child at more risk, but I can guarantee you that the parents will use those few days to "convince" the child to retract their statement alleging abuse. Just *think about it.*

Strength Through Association

It has been my experience that many victims need to know there are males that will *not* victimize them. Eventually they will learn to trust again due simply to that positive contact with a non-threatening member of the same sex that once terrorized them. There's no magic formula for making the victim feel more comfortable about what happened to him or her. What is important is the demeanor of the interviewer.

The same holds true for persons who were victimized by females. Developing a relationship with another female who does not exploit the victim can be very healing. For a good tag-team, there is nothing better than a friendly male cop and a friendly female advocate (or vice versa) to help develop the victim's beginning steps of learning to trust. By bonding with "normal" adults who will not victimize them, the victim can grow and heal.

Victims are simply people who were in the wrong place at the wrong time; the solution as to what they do with the remainder of their lives often lies in the hands of the individuals with whom they have significant contact immediately after the crime or after the crime is finally disclosed. Those "normal" adults may offer the magic of a "home base," someone to call when the victims are frightened long after the system has finished with them. It is knowing that five years later, they will still hear a friendly voice on the phone and that someone really cares about them as a human being.

Marie's Story

My name is Marie and my natural father molested me for four years, starting when I was twelve. Because my father and siblings are still alive, I am not identifying myself out of respect for some and fear of others who have threatened me, more than once, for disclosing the "family secret."

I am one of those kids who went through the system Don and Susan talked about. They "did it right" with me and I'm honored to have been asked my opinion about their work as well as offer some insights. The people that helped me "listened" and that is the key.

What I remember most was that once I got out of the home, in the company of safe adults, I was not treated "like an alien." I was treated like a person who had value, in spite of my background, the abuse, or my own acting out. Although I felt it unfair that I was the one sent to an institution (while my father was at home, watching cable television and sipping a cocktail) at least I was among other girls who had experienced the same thing; I wasn't alone, my "unseen deformity" was shared. Some of the girls in custody perceived it as punishment, but for the first time in years, I felt safe to sleep at night.

The court process was as they've described, and worse. I remember my first court date, when I was offered "a deal." Dad would relinquish custody and criminal charges would be dropped if I would recant the molestation; a deal for him, certainly not for me. Had it not been for the support I had in that courtroom, their eyes telling me they would stand behind me regardless of my decision, giving me the right to choose, I don't know what I would have done. I thought about how I felt the first time he raped me. It was real, it happened, it was horribly wrong, and physically painful. Knowing I could trust those *safe* individuals to be with me all the way, regardless of the outcome, I refused to recant and a court date was set.

At the trial, I remember being attacked by the defense attorney, who was trying to get just one juror to believe it was my "promiscuous behavior" (as a *child*) which was the reason and justification for my father raping me. When the jury found it easier to believe the lies, my father was not punished. I was victimized again, only this time by strangers. How I wished the judge, jury and especially my father could have felt what I did, (the rape and molestation) even if only for a minute or two. They would all have wept and given faithfully to child abuse charities thereafter.

It took years for me to stop being afraid, even after being placed in protective custody. My father is now very old and feeble, yet thoughts of encountering him still frighten me and I avoid any contact. However, with the approach police and social services took, the way they treated me, I did find that there *were* folks I could trust; a man that wouldn't molest me and a woman that wouldn't sell me out and both believed me. We actually could laugh and talk about other things. I didn't have to pretend to be "normal", I was normal. By bonding safely with Don, I learned that I didn't have to cling to a boyfriend for acceptance nor allow myself to be abused. I learned from Susan that you don't have to have sex with a man to make him love you. I learned from them, my foster parents and others, all the appropriate human survival skills that I should have been taught by my *father.* The only thing he taught me was how to be his sexual object and made me believe I had no power over my life, or my body.

I guess what meant the most to me were the adults... important adults who believed me, wanted to protect me, were available to me when I really needed them, and are still, fifteen years later, available to me as friends. They educated me; I learned that my behavior, fears and inability to trust were normal under the circumstances. After I became an adult, they included me in a discussion with another victim to give her hope. They gently allowed me to become stronger and develop self esteem. They gave me some power back over my life.

Dad's message to all of us kids, unfortunately still believed by some of my siblings, was that we were worthless. Well, I may never be anybody big and important, but I swear I will never be worthless. I will always be the good guy and I will raise my child to be good, to protect himself and to teach his children the same. I learned this profound message because some adults, "Did it Right" with me. I ask that as you approach every child who has been abused, to "do it right", give them belief, hope and the knowledge that they have control over their own life.

Marie, 1998

Author's note: Today, Marie is married, a mother, happy and loved. We are very proud of her.

DH/SDD

Statements You Don't Want to Hear - or Make

When a child has disclosed abuse to you, the important thing for you to do is to acknowledge that *you will report it and do everything possible to help* the victim be kept out of future harm's way. Do not make statements you can't guarantee, e.g., *"No one is ever going to hurt you again"* or *"I won't let Daddy ever hurt you again"* or *"We'll send the bad guy away to prison, and you'll never have to see him again."* I recall times that teachers, law enforcement officers and social workers have had to eat those words when the child was placed back in the home, or the perpetrator was neither prosecuted nor sentenced to serve time, but rather allowed to stay free, on probation—sometimes allowed to remain in the home with the child they abused.

At that point the child has been betrayed by those they loved, the person they trusted to stop the abuse, and by the courts. I think you can get the picture of how much that child will ever trust again—or why they would not bother to report again. But, let me give you a prime example of a case that should have worked; guarantees that *should* have been easy to make!

Case Study: "Little Bit"

An officer assigned to juvenile crimes, one with whom I'd worked on several cases, called me asking for assistance. In response to suspected molestation reports being filed by teachers, he was intermittently interviewing an eleven-year-old female who, he was convinced, was being incested by her step father, but was afraid to talk. The child, whom we shall call "Little Bit," would come very close to telling, then clam up. Officer "M" asked me to ride along one day, to speak to her Girl's Health class about my own history of abuse and triumph over tragedy.

I fell in love with Little Bit the day I met her; she had a big heart and a laugh that came from her toes. I *also* knew she was very sexualized, far beyond her years. She looked, dressed, talked and acted like a twenty-year-old prostitute. She was tough, mouthy and aggressive; her eyes gave away the fear and pain.

Two weeks later, Officer M called and told me that Little Bit was ready to disclose. He was going to school to take the report. Unfortunately, he already had firm plans to be on vacation for two weeks, but before he left, he wanted her to have a support system in place—me. Later that night, I met alone with Little Bit to prepare her for what the following few weeks might be like. After our meeting, a two-page report of additional information was faxed to Officer M. The perpetrator had been a busy fellow. Little Bit had many horror stories to tell him.

Officer M went to the school early the next day. Little Bit blew him away with her disclosures. He went immediately to her home to inform the mother. As is common in many incest cases, Mother denied the allegations and threw all of Little Bit's things on the sidewalk and in the yard during her half hour discussion with Officer M. Little Bit was taken to the shelter that day.

Her current stepfather was one of five, all but one of whom had molested her—with the mother's permission and encouragement. Mother traded Little Bit's services for "things" and "trips." In between husbands, mother would take Little Bit to bars; from the age of eight she had been prostituted by her mother for drinks. Little Bit had an incredible memory. She could put dates, times and places on almost every event. Officer M was excited; we had a good case.

Little Bit was concerned about her little sister remaining in the home. She knew "C" was being molested by the current step dad, but would not talk. Officer M delayed his vacation a day to go to school to talk to the little sister. She had new bruises all over her arms and face, but insisted that she "fell" and that "Little Bit was lying, and that nothing had happened to either of them."

Little Bit was placed in foster care and the perpetrator was placed in jail to await trial. Away from her mother and home environment, she began to change and spend time doing some positive thinking about her future. Little Bit was in the system almost two years before the criminal case went to trial. We had endured thirty-seven delays, postponements and trial interruptions. Ultimately, to save her own hide, Mother agreed to testify at the trial against the perpetrator in exchange for not being charged as an accomplice. The perpetrator was convicted of thirty-six felony counts of sexual activities with a child and was facing up to forty years of incarceration. He was sentenced to a whopping *nine* years. Little Bit sat in the court the day of sentencing and sobbed. She had been an incredible, irrefutable witness, but a sentence of nine years did not give her a sense that it was worth all she had been through. She still had months of hearings yet to come addressing the appropriateness of any contact with her mother.

Little Bit's Mother had to be threatened before she came to any dependency hearings or discussions *yet Social Services kept trying to place Little Bit back in the home.* Child abuse reports kept coming in on "C" from the school – several new bruising episodes, even after the perpetrator was placed in jail.

Officer M and I continually tried to speak with the social worker and Little Bit's court appointed attorney. They assured us that she would be *safe.* By the time a dependency hearing date was finally set, Little Bit had been in foster care and shelter homes over three years, had minimal contact with her sister by phone and saw her mother only at juvenile court hearings. Little Bit's grandparents would not talk to her "for all the terrible times she caused her mother to endure."

Finally, the day came for the juvenile court hearing to determine custody. Officer M and I met Little Bit's attorney that morning. He had never opened her file and was not familiar with what had happened to her. (Little Bit's court-appointed attorney may as well have been a fence post!)

I shall never forget that day in court, nor shall Officer M— and certainly Little Bit has not forgotten. After all the facts were presented, the judge called Little Bit to the bench. I sat in the front row to give her moral support for what I *thought* was going to be a victory day. Officer M sat in the back, waiting for the pronouncement. He expected that mom's parental rights would be terminated and Little Bit would be placed permanently into a good foster home, or possibly placed for adoption. We knew of two families that *wanted* her. The judge (her first month as a juvenile judge) smiled at Little Bit, then began the demise of a child—and a great juvenile cop. (These were her exact words— I wrote them down.)

"Little Bit, some terrible things have happened to you, so I am going to give you a choice*. You can continue to bounce from foster home to foster home until you are eighteen, never returning to your old neighborhood, or your friends at school, and continuing the loss of contact with your family. OR…You may return home to take care of your little sister, to make sure this doesn't happen to her. But, if you return home, I want you to feel free to call me or the police, if anything happens to you again." (**It was not a choice; it was a pronouncement of a life-sentence to "Little Bit."*)

I heard Officer M gasp from the back of the room; I thought I was going to throw up. Little Bit slammed the door shut on her heart, stared at the judge and said, "Yea, right, I'll call you. I'm going home. Nobody gives a damn anyway." The judge smiled, admonished Little Bit for using profanity and returned full custody, unmonitored, to the mother. Officer M was standing outside the tiny juvenile court trailer, screaming at the top of his lungs to Little Bit's attorney and social worker. To be honest, I was right there in the thick of it with him. Little Bit was walking toward her mother, tears running down her face. Mother was glaring at the child; the yelling began before the car door closed.

Officer M screamed at the judge, lawyer and social worker that day, "I'll never bring another kid into your stinking system – I quit!" And that he did. He is now an undercover narcotics officer, believing he'd rather deal with reality than the myth of juvenile protection.

I kept in touch with Little Bit over the years, encouraging her to keep the magic number of eighteen in her mind—then she would be free to live on her own and out of the nightmare. Mother had another live-in. The day he moved his things in, Little Bit pulled him aside and told him she would kill him if he touched her, or C. (She meant it.)

Little Bit has been actively involved in drugs and alcohol since the age of fifteen, with prostitution often her means of support. She has attempted suicide three times and has been in the hospital numerous times from being beaten by boyfriends.

The first time she tried to kill herself, we did get victim's compensation to have her hospitalized. She tried to commit suicide on Friday; on Monday morning they came in and told her that the benefits had run out, she had to leave. Little Bit never saw a mental health professional.

The Perp? When the time came for him to be released from prison, Little Bit asked me to inquire as to the jurisdiction into which he would be released. She was very concerned about running into him again. We checked with the California Department of Corrections and, to our surprise, learned that he had *never* been incarcerated. Oops! He *never* went to prison. Since he was never *ordered* to go, technically he didn't have to. When he left Chino after his placement evaluation, nobody had given him a reporting date or a prison to go to, so he had served his years, free as a bird. We were simply told, "There was a mix-up in the paperwork." To this day, except for the time he served waiting trial and during his confinement at Chino for an evaluation, he spent less time in the system than Little Bit did.

"C"? Pregnant at fourteen; father undisclosed. Married twice; at last contact she was living out of a car with two kids, surviving as a prostitute. (Teenage prostitutes have made the correlation between sex and self esteem. When they engage in sex acts for money, they are actually getting a "self-esteem fix." Since they equate their own self-worth as being attached to their allowing people to have sex with them, they are caught in a psychological addiction that is difficult for them to break.)

A long story, but one I felt could encapsulate many of the things that can go wrong in a case and how, even with the best of intentions of law enforcement and advocacy, sometimes the system simply fails.

Ignorance is Not Bliss!

Detective Howell has told you it's important to make the environment one of comfort and familiarity for a child. I believe it's *critical*. They don't have to have special rooms set up for a child, but the bullpen of a police station is certainly not the place!

Case Study: Sherrie

I was asked to take a child for an interview with a detective. Patrol had taken the initial report; the detective requested that the victim come to his office. Sherrie had not merely been molested; she had been violently raped, sadistically and repeatedly. In spite of the seriousness of the crime, our request for a private room was denied, and for her "interview" we were escorted into a crowded, noisy room with five officers, all on the phone or talking to other "visitors." (Some of the visitors were criminals, some victims and some were witnesses.) No private rooms, no cubicle dividing, no sense of privacy.

It was the detective's first week in the Juvenile Unit. The previous Friday, he had been investigating arson. He appeared to be *annoyed* that he had to take the time to interview Sherrie, and it took only minutes to learn that he knew nothing about juvenile sex crimes. The Detective kept saying, "I can't believe this, I can't believe it." Although only an expression to him, to Sherrie he was pronouncing judgment. He was rude, brusque and impatient; he kept barking at her to speak up (like she was the criminal).

Finally, he yelled at her saying "Speak up damn it, I'm trying to tape-record your *confession*." (That's another one of those opportunities to "Think about it.") I stopped the interview, told the officer I would be calling his supervisor to request another detective, and took the child home.

If you don't know about juvenile sex crimes, *learn before you traumatize a child.* (If you anticipate being transferred into juvenile crimes, but have received no training, at least *educate yourself.* In addition to this text, there is a bibliography at the end of this book. Any one of the titles suggested is a good place to start.)

One final comment about talking to a child. Adding to Don's remarks, size can be intimidating to anyone. Standing over a child, in your uniform, with a gun strapped around your waist, is not the best way to get the communication channels open. Some victims have been told by their perpetrators that they will be arrested if they tell, or that "daddy has police friends that will kill you if you tell." Imagine yourself being eight or nine, with that threat in your mind when someone six feet three is staring down at you asking you to tell. Additionally, supporting Detective Howell's statements, do not expect a child to sit quietly through an interview for an hour. They can hardly make it through a Disney movie. *Think about it.*

Is It the Truth, a Lie, a Fib or a False Memory?

It is so easy to believe a child, or an adult, is lying about things that we do not want to address as a society! Children lie to *get out of trouble*—not to get *into* trouble. I am appalled at the number of times I've heard that a police officer has called a child a liar. *Perpetrators come in all shapes and sizes, from every profession and walk of life.* They are not all seedy old men with rain coats who hang out in the bushes offering candy to children.

If the perpetrator is employed, respected, perhaps active in the community or has a high profile, child victims will be less believed than those who report abuse from a substandard family or living environments or a less well-to-do suspect. I know of several situations where a child recanted their disclosure, but it's usually after pressure from the family or, as in Little Bit's case, when they know that it will serve them no good to disclose. "Nothing will happen—no one will protect me, anyway." Those are painful words to hear coming from a child.

Did they make it up? Think of a child's imagination inventory. It is basically limited to what they have been exposed to. Rarely do we stop and realize that children lack the imagination inventory to make up stories that pass the litmus test of a good investigator. They cannot be aware of and tell the color, texture or smell of semen from any accidental adult channel surfing! Think about it!! Could any of you make up a good sexual escapade story? Certainly you could. As adults you have experience from which to draw and comprehension with which to embellish. A child's imagination inventory is blank in the area of sexual activity *unless they have experienced it personally.*

Are they lying? I prefer to ask a child if they are telling the truth or if they are telling a fib. The word "lie" usually has a punishment attached to it. A fib is forgivable and one they will more readily admit if the softer word is used. For the most part, however, it is vital that each of you start from a point of neutral belief. Unless something has changed in the last decade, I see no gain for *anyone* to come forward with stories of sexual abuse or rape.

Is it a false memory? While there are isolated incidents when individuals come forward with totally false accusations, (see False Allegations in Chapter 4), it has been my experience that rarely does anyone benefit from admitting being a victim of abuse. Certainly there is no glamour in admitting that you were used for an adult's sexual pleasure when you were four. Gagging on an adult penis when you were five is not a story that will win friends and influence people.

I am a survivor of sexual abuse. When my memories returned, the last thing I felt I wanted to do was tell anyone about the atrocities that were perpetrated against me. I knew there was a belief about incest survivors that would label me; I would be looked at or perceived differently.

I certainly was not prepared to be labeled a liar, which is what has happened to many adults who have come forward with stories of abuse. Many have been accused of having a false memory and told that somehow a therapist convinced the individual that these things happened to them. Not only is it discounting the victim, it is ludicrous! No one could have "programmed me or persuaded or led me" to believe the things that I remembered.

I've known a lot of therapists in my years of working with victims, many fine, talented respected individuals in the mental health profession. Not one of them could have convinced me, nor most of the other individuals with whom I share a common background. We were victimized as children and penalized for remembering as adults. False memories? Think of any other amnesia sufferer, like a car wreck victim or post-traumatic stress survivor such as a Vietnam Veteran. Their memories are real, correct? We celebrate and applaud when they regain their memories and start their healing. Then why aren't the memories of sexual abuse given the same courtesy?

In reality, adults who were victims of sexual abuse are quite good at filling in details that they could not have provided during the early years of their abuse simply because of a maturity level difference. Names and places are easy for a child to forget. But as an adult, tracking down the school they went to and identifying the teacher that molested them becomes much easier for them and allows them to provide accurate dates, locations and names. (An example: How many of you remember the name of your second grade teacher? Perhaps you can remember their face, but you may have even forgotten the name of the school you attended. However, if after thirty years it became important for you to know, you as an adult would know how to go about the fact finding.)

This fact gives more supportive reasons that the out-of-statute sexual assault victims could make excellent witnesses. The statutes of limitations are put in place because it is believed that *witnesses' memories fade over a period of years*. This is entirely untrue in the mind of a sexual abuse survivor who comes forward with their story twenty years after the incident, when it is finally remembered or they have summoned the courage to finally tell. Their memories have clarified, not faded, during the years of not telling.

Could it be we as a society are just too uncomfortable with the whole issue? *Think about it.*

Law Enforcement / Advocate Teaming Benefits

Most law enforcement officers pray for a witness to corroborate a victim's statements; however, many cringe when those witnesses are also victims of the same perpetrator or worse, the case has multiple offenders *and* multiple victims. Often you will have several families interested in, and demanding, justice. It is impossible for one officer to stay in contact with all of the families and victims, keeping them apprised of the status of the investigation. Parents and victims, however, do want to know what's going on, and deserve an update. This is where a qualified advocate can be your best resource.

With multiple families involved, you will be prevented from working the case if you are responding to ten or fifteen calls a day from all of the victims' families. Update the advocate and let them contact the families for you. The parties involved will appreciate being informed and you'll get to do your job. (Trust me, the victims' families don't care who apprises them, as long as they get frequent updates. It doesn't have to be the police officer!) Consider the qualified advocate as an unpaid extension of your own staff. You'll be glad you did.

There is an additional benefit to using an advocate in *any* case. Most officers don't like to think their credibility is questioned, but it is a fact that when the news is less than favorable, often the advocate can explain it in an easier and more palatable manner. For an officer to say, "I have insufficient information to prosecute," doesn't make the victims or their families feel any better, yet it is often all an officer can say.

An advocate can direct them to several resources for therapy, make suggestions for family healing, or give examples of similar cases where the case did not move forward for prosecution. It removes some of the isolation felt by the family and gives them something to feel other than *betrayed* or lay the blame for lack of prosecution at the feet of law enforcement.

Although most "teaming" benefits everyone involved, there are times when the system simply doesn't work and in spite of the cooperation of multiple disciplines, the system fails. "Day care" is a classic example.

Case Study: Multiple Offenders / Multiple Victims, "Day-care"

Next to a child homicide, I believe cases with multiple victims and multiple perpetrators are the hardest to work. I don't know anyone that will disagree with me.

I am reminded of a well-known day-care center case with multiple victims and many perpetrators which *should* have gone to a successful prosecution. However, every mistake that can be made in this type of case happened. A case with so many victims and so many alleged perpetrators had never been reported or received that kind of publicity. No one was trained or prepared to deal with a case of that magnitude. Every profession—law enforcement, mental health, media, social services, the courts and advocacy made gross errors. The following will provide some background information for those of you not familiar with the case, and examples of some of the errors that were made.

"Day-care" involved members of a family that ran a well-established day care business. Several children had been withdrawn from the school over the years due to the parents' suspicions that their child was being hurt or abused. Some phoned the police, most didn't. Some reports had been made over the years to Social Services which had been deemed "unfounded." Some parents called advocates groups but were not willing to "go public."

When it finally was formally presented to the police as a complaint, many advocacy agencies had already heard from several parents and some of the agency staff had been told that a few of the parents *participated* in the pornography aspect or used some of the other children sexually.

When allegations were finally sufficient to warrant an investigation, prior to any contact with the suspects, the jurisdictional police department sent a letter to *every* family who had a child at "Daycare," saying they believed their child may have been a witness to, or possible victim of sexual abuse. The letter was sent *ten days* before the first search warrant was issued and the police went to "Daycare." It was spotless when they arrived and no concrete evidence was found. Obviously, a week is plenty of time to remove evidence. First of many mistakes.

After several children suffered through the tales of horror, the mental health worker who was doing the evaluations simply "cut to the bottom line" with the subsequent victims, telling them she *knew* that certain things had happened and proceeded to list the incidents to the child that she had been told by other victims. The child would agree, then she would proceed with the specifics about that particular child. However, when watching the videotapes of the interviews, it was alleged that the therapist was *leading* the witnesses. She wasn't; she was simply getting the obvious out of the way. That contributed greatly to the lack of prosecution and convictions.

The parents who had victim children, and those who had left prior to the report being made, were experiencing tremendous guilt about not listening to their child, nor making any formal complaints (for those that had knowledge). Advocate groups determined that it would be good to allow the parents to come together to vent their frustrations and their guilt in a mental health environment. The *case specifics* were not allowed to be discussed. It was an opportunity to deal with feelings, only. Unfortunately, no tape recordings of those occasional gatherings were made. Bringing the parents together for support *sounded* like a good idea. By the time the case was close to trial, according to the defense, that between the mental health workers and the parents' gatherings, the children "had been brainwashed and the evidence was, as a result, contaminated."

During the course of the case, we learned that there were over fifty young adults who came forward and told of having been in "Day-care" as a child. They revealed that they had experienced the identical types of abuse and sexual crimes being reported by the current victims. Unfortunately, they were all "out of statute" and those who *wanted* to could not testify. (Out-of-statute means that the crimes against them had happened too long ago to be legally considered.) They were not allowed to give any deposition nor testimony which would have corroborated all of the current victims' stories.

One of the adult survivors of "Day-care", a journalist, was assigned to cover the trial. It was very difficult, but I will give that individual a great deal of credit. The news reports were impartial, but covering the trial necessitated that individual's return to therapy when it was over. The bottom line of "Day-care" is that great advocacy progress came out of the case and disciplines that had never before "teamed" learned that there were tremendous benefits to communication.

Similar cases with victims not being able to testify are not uncommon. Detective Howell and I worked one where several victims were willing to testify and could have made the case, but were not allowed to testify because their own abuse was "out of statute." Unfortunately, until the laws in most states are changed to allow out-of-statute victims an opportunity to testify, we continue to have them placed on the stand to testify—with a gag over their mouth, unable to make any reference to their own victimization by the accused. The truth, the whole truth and nothing but the truth? No, only the edited version of what they are allowed to tell.

Brainwashing a Child

"Day-care" presents an excellent opportunity to discuss *Brainwashing* a child. It was alleged in "Day-care," and in other cases, that the children had been rehearsed or brainwashed to tell the same stories, simply by repeating it to the child several times.

If we *could* brainwash our children by simply repeating the same messages frequently, they would all brush their teeth three times a day, keep their room clean and *always* do their homework. In a family environment it's called "nagging" instead of brainwashing—and it still doesn't work!

That's not to say that a child can't be rehearsed by one parent to have a string of sentences to say about the other parent, with no knowledge of the meaning. Our children recite the pledge of allegiance in school, and until the age of ten or eleven, half of them don't know what the words mean, and have several of the phrases wrong. Until third grade, my own children thought they were pledging "for Richard Stands" ("for which it stands"). That's the way it sounded to them over the loudspeaker at school. They could recite it, from beginning to end, just as a child (who has been scripted by a parent or someone in a position of trust) can do, but it will be flat, without emotion.

So, if a child sounds like they're saying the pledge of allegiance—flat, monotone, some of the words too mature for a child of their age, then you should ask them what each key words means. If there are holes in the story, that's where they will come out. A child (and often an adult) who has been a victim will tell you in steps, testing the water, garnering their strength. It took Little Bit years to tell me all of the things that had happened to her. They are painful experiences and seldom come out at one sitting. As your rapport with a child or any victim builds, and their trust level accelerates, you will learn more.

The Tape Recording Issue

There can be a strong downside to tape-recording the first few interviews since they may conflict greatly with the latter interviews as the victim learns to trust and becomes more comfortable imparting the information to you. If the conflicting tapes should happen to be available to the defense, it may be enough to create some doubt as to "which is the truth?" I have seen videotaping backfire in a few cases. As you will learn, in a felony trial it is the doubts and the unresolved questions that create opportunities for a mistrial or hung jury or a verdict of not guilty.

This is a good place to briefly mention the thirteenth juror rule or what is known as a "directed verdict." In California Courts, it is the responsibility of the jury to convict or not *based upon the prosecution's ability to use the evidence to convince the jury of guilt.* A directed verdict allows a judge to overturn a jury decision of guilty when the prosecution has failed to prove their case.

In the mid-eighties I worked on a case with several adolescent girl victims, many of whom made excellent witnesses. There had been some original taping made of the girls' preliminary interviews when two of them had initially denied that something happened. Ultimately, as their confidence in the law enforcement officers grew, they finally disclosed.

The case was an unusually ugly one with sexual acts that caused the jury to wince when told by the victims. From what the girls said, from the perpetrator's reactions, from every *sign*, it was clear that the man was guilty. *HOWEVER*, at the time the jury returned with the guilty verdict, once the courtroom quieted down, the judge had to impose the thirteenth juror rule and by issuing a directed verdict, overturn the jury's verdict. Based on the *facts* alone, the judge felt that the prosecution had not proven the verdict; doubt had remained, the prosecution had not proved beyond a shadow of a doubt. In spite of the testimony, the perpetrator's near admission of guilt and public sentiment that he was guilty, that Judge had no choice but to follow the law, overturn the jury's guilty verdict and set the man free. Since there were no unreported crimes or other victims, he was not tried again.

There are a couple of points to this story. Obviously, the first one is that regardless of how good you think your case is, there is *always* room for surprises. For that reason, I caution you against giving any child, or parent, *any* guarantees. The second reason is to illustrate that even the most minute of laws or rules may bite you firmly in the rear when you least expect it. Lastly, it strengthens Don's remarks about your written report containing all the information, correctly.

Even if you should be successful in a prosecution, there is *always* the chance of an appeal five years down the road. Victims move, they get on with their lives and witnesses die or forget. Someday it may be nothing more than the accurateness and completeness of your report that will sustain a conviction. The purpose of this book is to ensure that you will never regret that day.

"Who Told You What to Say?"

I separated this from the brainwashing section because it brought to mind another incident of miscommunication with a child and how they take things so literally. They often make great witnesses since they respond only to the apparent question and, unlike adults, don't ramble on with unrelated dialog. When familiar with the court setting, a child can make even a better witness.

For that reason, I took a very bright, articulate six-year-old for a courtroom tour a few days prior to the trial to prepare her to testify. As in many cases, the parents had been subpoenaed and would not be in the courtroom to give the child any support during their testimony. Any additional comfort we could offer the child needed to be put into place.

Working with a judge, we allowed the child to practice speaking directly into the microphone, sitting in the witness chair, talking to the Judge, knowing where the perpetrator was going to be, and to know where their support person(s) would be sitting.

During her "test run" in court chambers, she recited a nursery rhyme into the microphone, and the judge explained to her she could ask for water or ask to go to the bathroom. She was no longer afraid of going to court. On the way home, the mother and I both reminded her, as had the DA and the policeman earlier in the courtroom, to simply "Just say the truth."

The first day the child was called to testify, the defendant's attorney asked her: "Did someone tell you what to say?"

The child responded: "Yes."

Defense: "Who?"

Child: "My mom and Susan" (pointing to me).

The defense attorney went off on a diatribe about brainwashing or rehearsing a victim. It was a very tense moment in the trial. Fortunately, we had a judge who was very knowledgeable about children's thinking. He stopped the attorney and asked the child: "What did your Mom and Susan tell you to say?"

She responded: "The truth."

The perpetrator was sentenced to six years. A reminder to finish asking the question, which leads me to the next pothole on the road to justice.

Rush to Judgment

Things are not always what they appear to be, especially when you are dealing with a child. A very frightening but hilarious incident happened several years ago that illustrates the risk of accepting *any* isolated statement as "the *whole* truth" and why you should always ask the "and...?" part of a question to a child.

I received a panicked call one afternoon from a man I knew well, a *very* prominent man in our community, asking me to come to a particular school. At the time of the incident, his stepdaughter, whom I will call "Dottie," was five.

Dottie had a heat rash on her buttocks and on her vaginal area. The pediatrician told the parents to keep corn starch dusted lightly on her every day until it cleared up. I used corn starch on my own children's heat rash when they were little; time doesn't *always* change things.

Preparing for school that morning, Mom asked Step-dad to dust Dottie with the corn starch before they left. On the way to school, Mom tells Dottie that if she started hurting again, to tell the teacher. Around noon, Dottie is getting uncomfortable, starts wiggling in her chair.

The teacher asks: "What's wrong?"

Dottie responds: "My bottom hurts."

The teacher takes her to the bathroom and pulls down her underpants. White, moist, damp lumps are in her panties.

The teacher asks: "Who did this to you?"

Dottie responds: "My daddy."

The teacher asks: "Does your Mommy know?"

And the child responds: "Yes, she told me to tell you."

The teacher flies into the principals office and calls the police. *She* tells the patrolman *her* interpretation of the discussion and what she saw. (Yes, damp cornstarch does look like coagulated semen.)

The patrol officer calls the step-dad and demands he come to the school, without telling him why. They are repeating Dottie's conversation to dad and he is saying, "Yes, I put it there. Of course her mother knows. What is the problem?" Nobody was communicating. Neither the policeman, nor the teacher, asked Dottie what the white stuff was, or what *exactly* the step-dad had done.

In fairness, both the teacher and patrolman were relatively new at their jobs, and I admire them greatly for trying to protect Dottie with such gusto. It took about two minutes to straighten out the confusion, which I found terribly amusing. The cop and teacher were humiliated; dad did not, of course, see any humor in the event. He was thinking lawsuit. But the next day, he called the teacher to tell her that he was glad that she was paying attention and commended her for her willingness to take on someone of his stature in the community to protect a child. *Never* forget to ask that critical: "And...?"

Detectives Howell has another example of *"Getting it Wrong,"* an example of how the best intentioned officer can *"get it wrong" with dire consequences.*

One Sunday evening, patrol officers were called to the residence of a man we will call "Mr. Smith." Mr. Smith was divorced and had a four-year-old daughter whom he saw every other weekend. Mr. Smith had called the police department within a few hours of the end of his weekend visitation because his daughter had disclosed to him that "Mommy's new husband (*Mr. Jones* for purposes of this story) had fondled her vaginal area and when he put his fingers inside of her, it really hurt and burned." The child added that this touching took place while she was "on the rocking chair."

The court order required that the child was supposed to be delivered back to the biological mother and, as a result, would be in contact with the suspect. The officers, feeling that the elements of a child molestation existed, were left with a problem. They felt they had to do something to prevent further victimization of the child.

Their options were (a) to tell Mr. Smith to violate the court order, which he was reluctant to do, (b) take the child into protective custody, or (c) go to the home of the suspect and arrest him, thus removing him from the home and thereby protecting the child. The officers chose the latter. They went to the suspect's home and advised Mr. Jones of the molestation allegation. He denied the molestation, stating that at no time did he ever touch the child in a sexual fashion. He was taken into custody and booked into the city jail for child molestation.

Since Mr. Jones had a heart condition, the city jail would not keep him in that facility. He was transferred to the county jail where they had a medical facility and nursing staff that could watch him should he have a problem with his medical condition. Once at the county jail, he was booked in as a "child molester" where he had a series of negative experiences with both the jail deputies and other inmates.

The child was then returned to the biological mother with a stern warning from the patrol officers to never allow her husband back into the home because he might molest the child.

The patrol officers, in their opinion, had done a thorough job and were congratulated by their supervisors that night for conducting such an involved investigation, complete with an arrest of the suspect and seeing to the safety of the child.

Two days later, the reports were actually finished and processed through the police department's Records Bureau and came to my desk. Upon reviewing the report, I felt there were a couple of things missing in the interview with the child. I scheduled another interview with her. The mother, who was eager to resolve the molestation allegation, brought the child to my office for another interview on that very day.

I found the four-year-old to be very talkative and bright for her age. She was more than willing to trace hands and draw stick figures to identify body parts. When we came to the part of the interview where I was asking if the suspect had touched her on the outside of her vagina or the inside, using my fingers to demonstrate. (Refer to Illustration # 9, page 24.) She indicated that he had only touched her on the outside of the vagina and that it "burned like fire." I then asked her if the suspect was playing a game or if he was being mean to her when he had done this. She stated, "No, he was putting on the medicine." A few more questions revealed that the child had a medical problem and the family was putting over-the-counter ointment on her vaginal area to help clear up a rash. It is not unusual for these ointments to cause skin irritations and to "burn like fire" as the child indicated.

Upon talking with the child's mother, I learned this skin rash had occurred perhaps a year earlier and everybody in the family had "forgotten about it." The mother indicated that her current husband had, on occasion, helped to bathe and dress the child and, on a few occasions, had placed the ointment on her vaginal area. She also added that sometimes, in order to get the child to cooperate with having the medication put on her body, they would have her sit in her favorite chair (the rocking chair) and tried to play a game in order to get the ointment placed on the affected area with the least amount of struggling with the child.

I promptly arranged the release of the suspect from County Jail. He came into my office the following day and we talked about the child's statement. He did recall the rash problem the child had a year earlier, and ultimately he took a polygraph examination which indicated he had never been involved with any inappropriate sexual touching contact with the child.

CHAPTER 7

ODDS & ENDS OF "BUTTING IN"

Don and I have spent many hours together teaching, and it goes without saying that one of us usually has to sit quietly, anxiously waiting for the other to finish a subject so we may add our two cents' worth, a different perspective or another example.

Being part of the editing team, putting these two documents together, it was very difficult to not "butt in," and for the most part, I controlled myself. But, I have been given poetic license to do so in this section, an offer too good to pass up!

Don brought up several situations or suggestions that I'd like to expand on to further increase your knowledge and understanding.

Child Abuse Reporting

Don has given you the procedure for making the report. I have some thoughts I feel are necessary to enhance your effectiveness as a police officer, social worker, teacher, advocate or even a general member of the population at large.

Who is required to report? The reporting laws are very clear, and every individual pursuing a profession that deals with children should have it memorized! However, there are some situations where mandated reporters like Don, or me, learn of situations that have not been presented in a formal setting. Just because we are "off duty" does not affect the rule that we are mandated reporters, and as such, regardless of the hour or whether we are on duty or not, it is our responsibility to file a report with the Child Abuse Registry, as it is yours. Even though the law states you may not "have" to report when off duty, it is called "social and moral responsibility."

In dealing with the registry, I want to reiterate that you always want to follow the protocol by filing an oral report and follow with your concise written report. Get the name of the person who takes the report. Ask them to spell their name and ask who their immediate supervisor is, just in case you need to do a follow-up. Continue to check on the case. If nothing has happened, file another report. Wait two days and follow up by phone, asking what has been done, if anything. I cannot encourage you enough to *KEEP ON FILING* until something happens in that child's life to give you reason to believe that the slow wheels of justice have started to turn. Attending the funeral of a child who has been beaten to death is not a good way to close your file.

A good friend of ours, a marriage family and child counselor, just learned a lesson about reporting the hard way. With his permission, I'd like to share it with you.

The mandated reporting law states that if a professional has filed a report, subsequent professionals dealing with the same child are not required to file additional reports going over the same facts.

Our friend had a child referred to him by Social Services, accompanied by a copy of the original Child Abuse Report . He was to do an evaluation of the child and determine the validity of the child's allegations and to make a recommendation as to the appropriateness of the child staying with a particular parent.

To make a long story short, since the facts of the disclosure did not change during his several sessions with the child, nor did any new evidence surface, Dr. "A" did not file a subsequent CAR. He simply concluded his evaluation and forwarded it to social services

He was sued by the non-offending parent, charging that if he had filed the second child abuse report, the child would have been taken away from the offending parent more quickly. Unfortunately, in spite of having followed the mandated reporting laws to the letter, he still was successfully sued.

While I was the Director of the Adam Walsh Center, it was my policy that each of the case workers file child abuse reports, *even if they believed someone else had already done so,* most especially when we believed the child was at serious risk of harm. *Keep reporting, keep reporting, keep reporting until something happens.* Child Social Services agencies are understaffed, under-funded, have twice if not three times the average "workable" case loads. It is easy for any case to fall between the cracks. The squeaky wheel keeps pulling the case to the top of the mountains of files.

In the mid-eighties, there was a suspect convicted of multiple counts of incest against several of his children from three different wives. There had been over seventeen different reports made to the Child Abuse Registry and to teachers. No one listened to these children because of the prominence of their father in the community and his church affiliation and activity.

The abuse continued for years, and had it not been for one tenacious teacher who defied school policy (which was to let the principal determine whether a CAR report should be made — which is, of course, against the law), the children may have continued to receive sick, sadistic treatment at the hands of their father, with the obliging, passive or complicitous mother(s). The teacher ultimately lost her job, but she has stated that was a small price to pay to get the children out of that environment.

Due to lenient sentencing laws, the perpetrator is due to be released soon. His wife at the time of the trial, who was also convicted, was released over ten years ago and keeps filing to regain custody of her children!

There is a very sad commentary that should be a constant reminder for us to listen to children. Two teenage children in Orange County, California, were convicted (in the late-eighties) of killing their foster parents. During that same time frame, a similar incident happened in Montana where two teenagers were convicted of killing their natural parents. In both cases, the children had tried to get someone to listen to their stories of abuse in the home. Deaf ears were turned, follow-through was absent, or proof was not strong enough for action. Whatever the reason, at some point these children felt they had no way out but to protect themselves since the system was not going to do it for them.

In both cases, the young boys who were trying to protect themselves and their sisters, were tried as adults; the young females as co-defendants. Both were sentenced to prison terms. (A tragic side note:

The assistant district attorney who tried everything possible to prosecute the Orange County parents but was unable to build a solid case, had left the sex crimes unit and was reassigned to homicide. He was ultimately assigned the prosecution of the very child he had once tried to protect.)

Within a few years, the minor victims in Montana were granted clemency from the Governor and released. I believe the young men in California are still serving time.

While our statutes are clear about taking the law into your own hands, we are left to wonder if someone had listened to these children and pursued the reports, would the outcome had been different. Who is ultimately responsible for the death of the parents? Society? The system? Think about it!

Listen to the complaints you receive over the phone and read any report you receive a couple of times. Often, it is not just caseload that creates a situation where a child does not get protected. Sometimes, the report given is too vague if the caller is nervous or the individual taking the report may be buried with five calls backed up behind them. Here's a good example of all of the above.

Case Study: Unfounded
"Children neglected, undernourished, left unattended and being subjected to filthy home environment, living in deplorable condition with mother who is a crack whore, often the children at home alone for hours."

A grandmother called my office in tears one day. She no longer could tolerate what was happening to her grandchildren. Suffering with guilt about reporting her own daughter, she nonetheless gave the total picture of how these children, all three under five-years-old, were living. She felt they were not only being neglected and starved, she felt they were at great risk from one of the frequent gentlemen callers at the daughter's house. The children appeared to be very frightened of the man. The grandmother had tried to give the grandson a bath and was appalled at the bruises that covered his body and his sheer terror when she tried to place the child into the tub. The child kept screaming "Don't burn me again! Don't burn me again!" It was immediately after she left her daughter's home, after an unsuccessful discussion about the conditions in which they were all living, that she called to make this report.

She went on to say that the children lived in squalor; home empty except for a very badly stained mattress and a few cardboard boxes on the floor with their meager clothing and rotting food. After assuring her that she had done the right thing, I phoned the Child Abuse Registry with an official report and then called the jurisdictional police department with the identical facts and asked for a "wellness check" to be done.

The grandmother called several days later to say nothing had happened. The kids were still in the home; she was not aware of any visits by Social Services or by the police, and the children appeared to still be at risk. We kept calling Social Services and the police department to ascertain why nothing had been done. Finally, a week later, one of the filing clerks at the police department pulled the paperwork and read the report of the patrol officers who responded to our request to check on the condition and evaluate the allegations of neglect and endangerment.

They had gone to the residence *once* and knocked. Although they heard noises from inside, no one came to the door. They looked through the windows and seeing no one, they left the premises without making contact. Having seen nothing that first visit, they had not returned. (This particular jurisdiction has a "roll out only once" policy on child abuse reports.) The records clerk was kind enough to fax the police report. I sat stunned as I read the officer's statement regarding the call. The report read:

"After knocking with no response, we did look through the windows and it is our opinion that the house is no longer occupied. All that was visible was a mattress on the floor, a few cardboard boxes and a house that looked like it hasn't been clean in a year. No further action required to be taken. Copy of this report to Child Abuse Registry. End of report."

Obviously, something had been lost in the translation of the original report of concern regarding abuse, neglect and endangered children. The *very things that gave concern to the grandmother* were the things that gave the officers reason for no concern nor feel the need to return or pursue the matter further. Since a copy of their report was sent to Social Services, no further actions were taken by that department either.

Unfortunately, the mother died of a massive drug overdose, in front of these children, after being beaten and raped by her boyfriend. It was several days later when the grandmother went for another visit and found the terrified, starving children and the body of her daughter. If only one person would have read the full complaint report, perhaps they would all be with us here today.

Go that one extra step. If you have a child abuse report and you fail to make contact the first time, please give it one more try!

The Accommodation Syndrome

Don mentioned this behavior and it is important that you understand the full dynamics. Victims learn to accommodate—to accept bad behavior or treatment to stay alive, to stay in good graces or sometimes just to be able to eat or to protect a younger sibling. Their right to power over their own body seems to be taken away with that first attack, that first incident of sexual victimization. They accommodate to manipulate their surroundings into something survivable. *What they learned is that the only way to protect themselves is to be accommodating.* The right to ever say "no" again seems to have disappeared with the first assault. That accommodation syndrome explains why sexual assault victims will statistically have an average of five different molesters and often will have been the victim of a rape when an adolescent or adult.

Satanic Cult Victimization

Criminals have countless justifications to commit *any* crime. We know great atrocities have been committed under the name of God, Allah, Jesus, even Hitler or Charles Manson just to name a few. To some, any excuse will do. Some individuals believe Satan has told them to commit crimes, or they believe that in order to be a follower of Satan, they should commit a particular type of crime, and I personally happen to believe that these types of crimes happen. However, as to the scope, prevalence, magnitude, number of victims and why there is such a profound lack of evidence, I have no idea. But, I do not discount *all* of the reports nor consider them all to be false babbling of the mentally incompetent.

I believe that where there is smoke, there is at least a spark of fire, and I have heard too many reports from *credible* individuals, with firsthand experience, to not believe it exists, in some form, on some scale—somewhere. Perhaps it rests solely with the "dabblers" or the extremely perverted which extol their powers and terrify victims with horror stories. In time, we will know more about these situations. Or, we will learn that we have simply been the targets of a gigantic hoax. Either way, we will know.

Strength Through Association

One more quick comment about victims having to relate to someone of the same sex as their attacker. A current case involves a young teenage girl who has been incested for years by her stepfather and has a passive, non-protecting mother who has turned on her daughter since the report of the incest.

One cold afternoon, the investigator handling her case was close to her shelter at lunch time and remembered that she loved a particular type of sandwich. He dropped by to just give her a hamburger. She broke into tears. A man had taken advantage of her for years, exploited and used her, always expecting her to perform for him. Yet here on the porch of the shelter was another man, the cop who handled her case, who only wanted to give her a hamburger because he cared—not because he expected anything. In that simple gesture of thoughtfulness, she had learned there are men who will be kind to her without expecting sex in return. This incident was a pivotal point in her own healing.

THIS PAGE INTENTIONALLY LEFT BLANK

CHAPTER 8

ADVOCACY FOR ADULT VICTIMS

The Role of the Adult Advocate

Advocates' roles with adult victims vary only in the physical aspect of what you are able to do for them. The goal is still the same: to preserve any legal action and to meet the psychological needs of the victims.

One of the greatest benefits I feel I've offered to adults is to reassure them that they are not alone, that they are not responsible and *that they can heal.* Having a sympathetic, nonjudgmental, understanding ear of an advocate is the best resource an adult can have. Knowing someone believes you and is not shocked nor disgusted by the disclosures is a major part of healing. As part of my work with any victim, regardless of age, I stress the importance of therapy and have several professionals in whom I have great confidence in their ability to deal with victims of sexual abuse.

As Don mentioned earlier, often with adults it is an advocate, friend or relative that brings the case to law enforcement's attention. We are less frightening, less intimidating and we subject the victim to a first contact that is less than the black and white "just the facts" approach that police officers are required to glean from their interview.

Adult victims are not always the ones against whom the crime has been perpetrated. The *parents* of any child who has been molested, raped or kidnapped are also victimized, and traumatized. For them, often there is little support or attention given, yet they are equal in their amount of agony over the incident, albeit a different type of pain. They need someone to listen to their concerns, to explain what is happening, to tell them what to expect from the system, and what to anticipate as to the victim's behavior and future needs. Often, the greatest comfort I have been able to give an adult survivor is the knowledge that there is hope for a normal life after their healing has begun.

I remember, with a chuckle, about an adult survivor of sexual abuse who knew that she, like many survivors, had a disproportionate amount of rage and anger which would continue until her healing was complete. She called me one day at the Center, crying, talking about her explosive relationship with her teenage son. She felt that it was because of her unresolved emotional issues (which she perceived as "weaknesses") that she was so intolerant and angry with him.

She was greatly relieved to learn that I, as a mother, having nothing to do with being a survivor, had asked my own teenage son if he "wanted to live to be old enough to vote" during one of our many confrontations, as is normal between a mother and a six-foot fifteen-year-old.

Happy to know that others sometimes feel the same way about their teenagers, and laughing as we concluded, she was able to put her role as a mother into perspective and realize that not everything in her life revolved around being a survivor. This is a powerful example of what an advocate can do—where else would she have felt comfortable calling, admitting that she had moments where she mentally wanted to beat her child to a pulp without being considered an abusive mother?

Additional support can be given to an adult through your mere presence during a rape exam, in court, during law enforcement interviews and one of the most frightening, to accompany the adult to a lineup and give them arms into which seek assurance after the traumatic event and drive a very shaky victim home.

Case Study: Kathy

There are times when even the most seasoned advocate faces a day from hell they never forget. I had been working with an adult survivor in her forties who had just started to remember some of her abuse. She had always remembered "the basics" but knew there was more. Kathy had seven years of her life totally blacked out, but was doing well in therapy.

She was feeling quite empowered, even wanting to report her stepfather because thirty years after her incest, he was still teaching children in Sunday school, had new young stepdaughters, as well as granddaughters to whom he had access.

One night I received a frantic telephone call from her husband. Although two in the morning, he did not feel that "Kathy" could wait until the following day for support and he could not reach her therapist. Her memories were coming in terrifying waves; she was in the closet, sobbing and screaming and would not let him near her. Dick did not know what to do. He could not get Kathy to come to the phone, so my husband and I drove to San Bernardino.

Kathy was still seeking solace in the closet, but did allow me to join her. Similar to labor pains, the memories would come with gradual intensity and clarity. Kathy's eyes would get huge, she would moan, or sometimes in sheer panic scream, "oh my God, oh my God." When the memory of that particular event was fully recaptured she would collapse in a pile, sobbing on the floor or in my arms.

If she hadn't done so during the memory capture, eventually she was able to talk after the episode, and would tell me of the horrific incident she had remembered. She would approach the end of that incident, and a new memory would start, creating the horror and pain again. (This type of recall is called "flooding" in mental health literature.) The earliest memories were the least traumatic. As the night wore on and the early shades of morning peeped through the windows, Kathy was remembering being held down by her mother on the kitchen table while her father raped her — at eight years old. If she screamed or tried to get away, the mother would dump pepper in her eyes.

At eleven o'clock the following morning, after twenty minutes with no new memories, or warning signs of same, Kathy and I left the closet. All I had been able to do was hold her, cry with her, listen—and believe. We called her therapist and scheduled her for the first available appointment.

The catalyst to this event had been the expected arrival of her mother who was coming that day to talk about permanently living with them. A widow, she was having trouble making ends meet and Dick had invited her to share their home, completely unaware of her mother's participation in the sexual assault.

As I had listened to the torture Kathy endured, not only at the hands of her father, but with the knowledge and participation of her mother, I was *very* angry at two people I had never met. As my husband and I prepared to leave that morning after Kathy was final able to sleep, a very aged woman walked to the door. Imagine the conflict you would feel knowing that the very tiny, gray-haired frail woman being introduced to you was once a monster and now barely remembered her own name or was able to walk.

Did she move into their home? No. After Dick learned the specifics of her participation, and even realizing that the very sick, sadistic unprotecting mother was long gone, he decided that it would not be in Kathy's interest to have the mother reside with them. He arranged for her to be placed in a very nice, local elder care facility where Kathy could see her, when and if she wanted to, but feel comforted that her mother was being taken care and experience no guilt. Thoughtful husband. Smart move.

Somewhere, deep behind the mother's eyes, Kathy would occasionally see the woman that so terrified her as a child. She was glad she could walk away and leave her mother in competent hands other than her own, feeling strong enough to return only on her terms. Before she died, her mother did apologize to Kathy, but all she would say is, "I'm sorry for the terrible things that happened to you as a child." That was enough for Kathy. She didn't *need* the apology; she needed the validation of her memories.

CHAPTER 9

THE MOBILE MOLESTER / SEX CRIME PERPETRATOR

Earlier, Don gave you an example of a significantly older woman involved with a young boy sexually. Remember when he told you that the school had knowledge of her inappropriate activity with her male students, past and current? Unfortunately, this is not an uncommon situation. Rarely is there a prosecution where the suspect has not been previously "relieved" of their jobs or volunteer work without a formal complaint being made, or a note put in their personnel file which would protect children at any future employment site. That is an outrage against children.

It has been well publicized that molesting Catholic priests get moved from one parish to another after disclosure of molestation. Rather than be up front with the information and intervene on behalf of the victims in their church, they simply move the priest to another unsuspecting parish without any word of warning to the officials in the area into which he is being transferred. I want to be very clear that churches are not the only establishments guilty of this kind of activity. Schools do it. Mark Poteet, a janitor convicted of several molestation counts in the early-eighties, had been "transferred" from at least seven different schools for his inappropriate involvement with students prior to him finally being charged and convicted.

After a disclosure, many volunteers at children's groups are simply told their services are not wanted and released to prey on other children. However, when the unsuspecting new group calls for a reference, since nothing official was ever documented or pursued (and the information usually kept close to the chest of management), only the most glowing remarks about the individual by a clerk in the personnel department are made. There is no federal registry of child molesters. They can move from city to city, state to state, and with the system so backlogged (assuming an employer or nonprofit group even checks), it could be six to eight months before the individual's history surfaces and unless a prosecution took place, there will be no cautionary remarks that would warn any new prospective employer or group. Teachers moving from other states can obtain a temporary teaching position in most states while their background check is being conducted; often this background check takes eight months to a year.

If the state they moved from does not have a sex offender registration program, or the offender was simply let go rather than doing the morally responsible thing by reporting and/or prosecuting, teachers, priests, youth workers and volunteers continue to move freely about this country leaving behind a trail of victims. It is my wish, and Don's, that at some point before we pass, that we place as much value on the safety of a child as we do "reputations" of establishments, embarrassment at making a wrong choice for an employee or, most especially, giving a child's rights equal value with that of an adult offender. Rapists, for the most part, have the same mobility as child molesters.

It *is* called the *criminal justice system*—not the *victim's justice system* for a reason. Stolen cars can be tracked from anywhere in the country, even out of the country, yet we have no easily accessible central registry for individuals who are a threat to society. Do cars have more value than people? Apparently. It was only in the mid-eighties that a national missing childrens' registry was created, and in order to do so, we had to champion using part of the system that tracks cars. Some states still do not have a missing children's registry!

Think about it!

CHAPTER 10

DOMESTIC VIOLENCE

Something else for you to think about: It has only been in the last century that women have been thought of as more than chattel. Children have not yet obtained that level of recognition. If a wife is battered, it is called domestic violence. If a child is battered, it is called child abuse—the reference to the domicile, the "sanctity of a man's home," is completely removed from the charge. Years ago, whatever a man did to his wife and children was ignored. They were, like his mule, simply property to do with what he chose. Unfortunately, it takes an individual to die, usually one of prominence or one whose family is able to garner great media coverage, before our laws are changed. Nicole Brown Simpson was not the first wife to be battered and killed in this country. Adam Walsh was only one of thousands of children in this country that have been kidnapped and murdered. However, their deaths were not in vain; the system is slowly starting to respond.

Domestic violence shelters have been around for years, struggling, trying to get the population at large to recognize the scope of the problem. Their population of children is equal to that of wives. Child abuse is not a separate issue from domestic violence; it has just not yet been included in that category. A man's home is still a sacred place and children are the silent victims. They don't vote, they don't pay taxes, and for the most part, do not have a voice. It will happen; if you, the individuals reading this book, recognize that child abuse within the home is domestic violence regardless of the age of the victim, we are well on our way.

SPOUSAL ABUSE - EXTRA PROTECTION

This is a program worth duplicating and another great example of advocacy and law enforcement working together. While at the Center, I received a call from a local cop who was tired of taking "missing persons" or "parental kidnapping" reports from spousal abusers simply wanting to find out where their wives had fled and were using the system to track them down. (Shelters have the legal right to not disclose to a law enforcement officer if someone is residing at their facility.)

In our immediate area, we have seven battered women's shelters and, like Don said, the locations of those remain a secret for that very reason—they are supposed to be safe havens. In states where they are not kept secret, you have all read about murders that have happened on the front steps of a shelter!

We developed a great plan where police, the Center and the shelters worked together to assist law enforcement while keeping the whereabouts of victims secret, upholding the integrity of the purpose of the shelter. Eventually, fourteen different law enforcement agencies used that service.

In cooperation with the shelters, I was given a designated line to a phone at their facility (with no traceability to the shelter) for purposes of this project. All of those telephone numbers were typed in a random fashion without any identifiers. When a woman was reported missing by her husband (with no signs of foul play, of course), the law enforcement agency phoned the Center with her name and those of her children if she had taken them with her.

A call would be then be made to every one of the telephone numbers of all of the shelters, stating that I was trying to ascertain the safety of a particular individual, giving the name and those of any children. I never knew to whom I spoke nor which shelter I was calling since the designated number was simply answered with "hello." As soon as the names were spelled, and my name or the name of the staff person in my office making the inquiry was given, the conversation would terminate.

After calling all seven, I would wait for a call back. Generally the "missing" woman would call me, tell me she was safe, had not been kidnapped, her children were with her and that she was in an unidentified shelter. If the woman was at the shelter but too afraid to talk, an unidentified staff person would give me that information. I could then call the police officer back, tell him that the woman was in "some" shelter. Even if questioned or called as a witness, I would not be able to disclose her whereabouts, nor could I give it to the officer. I simply didn't know and could swear to that under oath. Nobody knew anything except that the woman had fled from abuse and law enforcement was no longer being used as the vehicle for a batterer to track down his punching bag wife.

This program also was beneficial when a man would report his wife as "missing" when in fact law enforcement believed he may have done something to her and was trying to cover his tracks. If we heard nothing back from the shelters within twenty-four hours, we could safely assume the woman was not a resident and the police officer could pursue other avenues for locate purposes.

If you don't have a program like this in your community, think of starting one. It doesn't cost a thing and will certainly make your job easier. You'll be glad you went that one extra step.

THIS PAGE INTENTIONALLY LEFT BLANK

CHAPTER 11

ADVOCATES WANTED – LOW PAY, LONG HOURS

I have been called many things in my lifetime, but one of greatest of those is "an advocate." I have been referred to as a pain in the rear (although not with such kind terms), a busybody, an interloper, a zealot, an intruder, an interfering bitch, a community watchdog and a bleeding heart, just to name a few. But, in time, I became thought of as a competent, knowledgeable friend of the courts, law enforcement and, most importantly, the victims. I earned that reputation because there are lawyers, cops, judges and social workers that did not intimidate easily *and had the courage to admit they could not be everything to everybody.*

This section of the book will give you some additional ideas how *an advocate* can provide the "Care and Nurturing of Victims." For law-enforcement officers, it is our intention that you use this chapter as a tool to ensure that you have balanced the rights of the victims with those of suspect. When law enforcement and advocacy work together on cases, both come away knowing they have done everything possible for the victim, helping to seal the cracks in the system whenever possible.

Advocacy is not as rare now as it was in the late-seventies and early eighties. The caliber of people available has been greatly improved. Training is mandatory and dedication is very high among those who commit their lives to being a friend to someone who has suffered.

Advocates are in the best of all places; they talk to law enforcement, the courts, the child, the social worker and the parents. *They are the central information repository* and can be a critical adjunct to your investigation. Reluctance to use an advocate limits your talent and is not always in the best interest of the victims. Besides, there are plenty of victims to go around—they don't need to be hoarded or kept in isolation. It is up to you to find an advocate with whom you can comfortably work. They do exist and are not at all hard to find. Ask any cop about the community "watch dogs."

Here are a few examples of how you can use advocates:

Responding to an "anonymous caller," advocates have packed courtrooms when the prosecutors had doubts that the perpetrator would get the length of sentence available. Often in child abuse cases, there are many people present who are friends and supporters of the perpetrator; rarely are there many present that give the clear message to the judge that the rights of the child are as important. Advocates can step outside the confines of the limitations of the system.

Advocates have provided transportation for parents (and children) to and from the countless visits to the prosecutors or detective's offices and sit patiently with them in the halls of courtrooms waiting for their turn to be called. Advocates have saved the jobs of parents who have been required to take time off of work for numerous appearances in court but have been unable to muster the courage to tell their employer that their child was victimized.

Advocates have argued with teachers and principals about allowing a child an opportunity to make up a test they missed while in court testifying. Advocates have held the hand of a rape victim during an exam they were unable to face alone. Advocates have spoken with other victims and shared firsthand experiences —and given hope. Advocates have turned the tide of a trial by their mere appearance. Advocates can sit in on a court proceeding or an interview and pick up information you may miss because they are focusing on the broader perspective.

Advocates have assisted in missing child cases, from distributing the flyers and coordinating the search, to obtaining the food for all the searchers. Advocates have accompanied parents to identify their child's body and make funeral arrangements. Advocates have given reassurance to countless prosecutors and cops who lost a case—or a child.

Using Advocates to Defuse
an Explosive Situation

Advocates are great educators. Using their talents and willingness to help, they make your job easier and lessen the impact on victims! They can do things that would get you fired! They are passionate, dedicated and willing to share their viewpoint or experience. I have been a guest lecturer at three colleges for over ten years, taught at POST courses, spoken at conferences and PTA's and at countless groups who wanted to know, to learn, to be proactive rather than reactive. Over 14,000 individuals have heard me talk about crimes against children, survivors, perpetrators, laws and how to protect a child. The population is hungry for information, and as long as there is an audience, I shall continue to try and educate and change the tide for the life of any child. One of my greatest audience opportunities came in the middle of a crisis.

When a priest was identified as a molester of many of the altar boys in a parish, the large church was dividing into two factions and the tension was escalating. The children who told, and their parents, were being revictimized, targeted for insults, being isolated and shut out of the very place they had expected would offer comfort. Putting together an attorney, a detective, a mental health worker and a prosecutor, we conducted a three-hour workshop at the church to address the issues and defuse the tension (without talking specifically of the case at hand). Why? Because the children in the church school were being torn apart by the parents' discomfort and lack of concrete information about molestation, the victims and the perpetrator.

The church counselor opened the meeting by saying that there are some things even God can't handle alone. (Smart man!) All of us who spoke that night were advocates, regardless of our professions. We made a difference in the lives of those children and the parents and caused bonding in the church instead of tension. The priest who molested? Convicted and sent to a special facility for priests in Albuquerque, New Mexico. Within two years he kidnapped and molested another boy. He is currently in prison for that crime, serving a first sentence with more than thirty reported victims for whom the bells of justice never rang.

Finding an Advocate to "Team with"

Most states have a victim witness program or a Court Appointed Special Advocates group (CASA). Many communities have small groups of advocates that have emerged from local tragedy. I encourage you to seek them out, find one or two that you have confidence in, and include them as part of your investigation process. It will probably be one of the best decisions you make in your career.

CHAPTER 12

PROFOUND SILENCE

Whether you are law enforcement officers, teachers, probation officers, lawyers, mental health workers or advocates, working with victims can be one of the most fulfilling careers possible. It is gratifying, frustrating, exhausting yet exhilarating. There is a common thread among those that commit their lives to working on behalf of those less fortunate; they have great compassion for others. Oddly enough, that very trait will often put them in a position of feeling isolated and unable to communicate their feelings about haunting cases—those where they wonder if they could have done something different and possibly changed the outcome.

For that reason, there is significant bonding between individuals who *can* talk at length about a child's murder or trade "black humor" stories about a current case to another person who shares the same concerns or has walked that path. It is a special bond and openness of communication.

During some intimate, cathartic conversations, I have learned that many of the other individuals with whom I have worked over the years share the same agony. *We rarely know the final outcome of most of the cases we've handled.* We may see a case through to successful prosecution, or see the child taken out of the home and placed in foster care, or in rare circumstances, return a child to an out-of-state parent they have not seen in ten years. From that point, we experience the void—the *profound silence* of not knowing the outcome.

For a moment in history we made a significant difference in that child's life, but we never get to read the end of their book. Did it turn out well? Were they happy? Are they still acting as victims or did they heal?

Most of the time we *never* know and the soft strains of the brief musical memory of those little ones fill our silent hours.

Wherever all of you children are—we have not forgotten and this book is dedicated to each of you. Thank you for helping us teach others.

SDD

EPILOGUE

As stated in the early pages of this textbook, this has been written as a basic "How To" tool. Many years of experience have been consolidated into what we think is an appropriate level of information for any officer to comfortably engage his or her first interview with a victim, regardless of age.

Since we anticipate continual changes in laws and local policies, we expect this handbook to be revised many times. It is our hope that you will contact us should you have any questions or advise us when a technique has been particularly useful, or with ways you've improved our suggested techniques.

Getting it All

We've spent a lot of time trying to teach the readers how to go about "getting it all", among other things. But now is the time to tell you that this is a lofty and therefore unattainable goal. Perhaps we should have been telling you how to get as close to this goal as is realistically possible. An example might explain it best.

Suppose that your best friend took a month long vacation to Europe and toured several countries during a nonstop attempt to see the entire continent. Upon his return the two of you get together for lunch and you ask your friend to tell you "everything" about his trip. Your friend then talks for more than an hour about "everything" that happened.

Two weeks later you have lunch again and this time your friend tells you additional facts about his trip. Two weeks later, at another lunch, the same thing happens. Does this mean that your friend lied to you during your first lunch? I think not. Instead he just added some stories that he hadn't thought of the first time or he simply didn't have time to "tell everything" during the first lunch. In reality you will never hear about everything that happened during that month.

Now consider a child who was molested three or four times a week every week for several years. Are we ever going to be able to GET IT ALL? Again I think not.

If at some future date a defense attorney asks you a series of questions such as "Have you received training in how to interview witnesses?" "Does that training teach you how to get ALL the facts?" And "Are you trained to write all of those facts down in your police report?" (I think you can see where I'm going with this.)

If you find yourself in such a situation, remind the District Attorney of the hypothetical trip to Europe and see if the D.A. can find a way to use that story to rehabilitate you as a witness and bring a very important point home to the jury.

APPENDIX A

Rape Trauma Syndrome

Victims of rape suffer a significant degree of physical and emotional trauma during the rape, immediately following the rape and over a considerable time period after rape. The symptoms that are consistently felt over and over by rape victims are clustered into a group and classified as the rape trauma syndrome. This syndrome has two stages: the immediate or acute phase, in which the victim's lifestyle is completely disrupted by the rape crisis, and the long-term process, in which the victim must reorganize this disrupted lifestyle.

During the acute phase, the rape victim experiences both emotional and physical reactions. The primary emotional feeling expressed is the fear of physical injury, mutilation and death. These symptoms are an acute stress reaction to the threat of being killed, and it is this main feeling of fear that explains why victims develop the rape trauma syndrome.

Although the immediate emotional reactions of rape victims vary, there appears to be two general categories of emotions shown: expressed or controlled. The victim displaying the expressed style will demonstrate feelings such as anger, fear and anxiety while the person showing the controlled style masks their feelings and displays a calm, composed outward appearance. Also during the acute phase, many victims report feeling irritated with people in the first few weeks after the rape and are prone to mood swings such as depression and emotional outbursts. The victim might also experience feelings of humiliation, degradation, guilt, shame, embarrassment, self-blame, anger and revenge. The victim finds that although she tries to continually block the assault from the mind, it keeps coming back.

Besides the immediate emotional reaction during the acute phase, the person also displays physical reactions. Because rape is forced sexual violence against a person, victims describe a wide gamut of physical reactions. Some victims describe a general feeling of soreness all over their bodies, while others specify the body area of the assailant's force. Other types of physical reactions during the acute stage include sleeping and eating pattern disturbances. In terms of sleep disturbances, rape victims have considerable difficulty with disorganized sleep patterns, complaining that they cannot fall asleep or find they wake up during the night and are not able to fall back to sleep. Victims who have been attacked while sleeping in their own beds might awake each evening at that time again and find they cannot fall back to sleep. Also, it is not uncommon for victims to scream out in their sleep. Eating pattern disturbances include such complaints as a decrease in appetite, stomach pains or remarks that the food doesn't taste quite right.

The second stage of the syndrome is the long-term process during which the victim must reorganize their disrupted lifestyle. The rape represents a disruption in the lifestyle of the victim, not only during the immediate days and weeks following the incident, but well beyond that to many weeks and months.

The victim has to cope with various symptoms during the long-term reorganization process. Changes in lifestyle is one of the symptoms. The rape often upsets the victim's normal routine of living. Many victims are able to resume only a minimal level of functioning even after the acute phase ends. Some victims go to school or work but are unable to be involved in social activities, while other victims respond to the rape by staying home or venturing out only with a friend.

Also included many times in the lifestyle change is a strong desire to get away, and a common response is to turn for support to family members not normally seen on a daily basis. Changing residence specifically because of a rape is another common response during this period of time. Many victims also change their telephone number, requesting an unlisted number.

A continuing problem from the acute stage is the occurrence of dreams and nightmares. During the second phase, victims typically report two types of nightmares. The first type of dream places the victim in a similar situation as during the rape. During this dream, the victim tries to get out of the situation that led to the rape but fails. The second type of nightmare occurs as time progresses, and the dream's content is still filled with horror as the rape victim sees themselves committing acts of violence against other people. Although the power in this second type of dream may represent mastery, the victim still has to deal with this violent self-image.

Another common psychological defense of victims during the long-term process stage is the development of fears and phobias specific to the circumstances of the rape. Victims will develop phobic reactions to a wide variety of circumstances. These include the avoidance of crowds, fear of being alone, intense feelings of insecurity and disillusionment regarding the victim's safety in the world. The rape victim might also find that they might have diminished sex drive or a fear of sex. This is especially upsetting if the victim has never had any experiences before the rape. The victim might find a general loathing for their body, feeling that it is their fault that the rape took place. Fears might also be specific to the characteristics of the assailant. For example, the victim might become anxious of the odor of alcohol, gasoline or cigarettes if the rapist possessed such an odor. A female rape victim might also find that she has acquired a generalized fear of men.

There are two variations of the rape trauma syndrome. The first of the two is called the compounded reaction to rape, during which the victim experiences not only the previously noted symptoms but also a reactivation of symptoms of a previous existing condition such as a psychiatric illness. The other variation is called the silent reaction to rape during which various symptoms occur but without the victim ever mentioning that a rape had occurred.

Counseling of rape victims is based on the following assumption: That the rape represents a crisis which disrupts the victim's lifestyle in four areas—physical, emotional, social and sexual. Victim counseling is an issue-oriented crisis treatment model with the focus of the initial interview and follow-up being on the rape incident, and the goal being to help the victim return to their previous level of lifestyle as quickly as possible. The victim is viewed as needing emergency services and the rape is viewed as a crisis situation. Previous problems not associated with the rape are not considered priority issues for discussion in the counseling. Additional professional help is needed for victims with compounded reactions.

APPENDIX B

Indicators of False Allegations of Sexual Assault by Strangers

In a seminar conducted by Roy Hazelwood, of the FBI's Behavioral Studies Unit, the following characteristics were reported as having occurred in enough falsely alleged cases of sexual assault by a stranger to be significant. These circumstances do not prove false allegations. When the case is looked at in its entirety, these characteristics could indicate a false allegation.

I. The Victim

A. The underlying motive for false allegation is a need for attention.

B Look for a disruption in family life.

C The victim suffers from low self-esteem.

D There are interpersonal problems with someone important in their lives.

E. Distress or positive events in recent life/stressful occurrences.

F There may be a history of undiagnosed illness (e.g., constantly going to the doctor with ailments that are false).

G. The victim may have made similar complaints in another area (usually of prior residence).

II. The Allegation

A. The report may be delayed and/or reported to someone other than law enforcement.

B. The victim may be indifferent to her injuries.

C. Details may be extremely detailed or extremely vague.

D. When interviewed, the victim will attempt to steer the discussion away from areas dangerous to her. (i.e., information you need to prosecute someone, location and/or description of suspects).

E. The victim will attempt to steer you toward safe areas as the amount of force used and her resistance.

F. There may be no reluctance to have her wounds/injuries photographed by someone of the opposite sex.

G. The suspect(s) may be multiple assailants or a single assailant who is huge and overpowering.

H. The suspect may be described as a total stranger or a friend of an unrecalled friend.

I. The sexual acts will not be outside the victim's normal repertoire.

J. Defense wounds will be inconsistent with the reported angle of attack.

K. Violence reported is vigorously physically resisted.

L. Injuries may be reported with indifference.

M. More serious wounds are in areas normally covered by clothing. Less serious injuries are in areas normally exposed.

N. Wounds do not involve sensitive areas of the body. They can lead up to the sensitive area but will stop short.

O. Messages may be carved in the body. (This never has been done in a righteous sexual assault.)

P. Wounds are either horizontal or lateral on the body.

Q. Wounds are anatomically oriented (usually the breast area).

III. Evidence

A. Damage to clothing is inconsistent with the report.

B. Damaged clothing is clothing that is usually not worn by the victim e.g., old clothes.

C. The victim "just now" recalls prior occurrences such as obscene phone calls or messages.

D. The scene does not support the story.

E. Notes allegedly left by the suspect are "cut and paste" or block letters that are usually threatening or sexually obscene. The note looks like something out of the movies.

F. Reported break-ins where there is theft or damage to property.

IV. Other Considerations

A. The victim may attempt to establish a relationship with the investigator.

B. The victim may claim, "You are not asking the 'right' questions."

C. There may be an abnormal dissatisfaction with the investigator.

D. There may be a continuous recall of additional facts.

E. There may be an apparent lack of interest in the investigation.

V. Recommendations

A. Don't confront the victim until you are convinced the allegation is false.

B. The victim should be confronted by someone other than the case agent, preferably the case agent's supervisor.

C. Use an empathetic approach.

D. Don't release information of the false allegation to the press.

APPENDIX C

THIS OUTLINE MAY BE CUT OUT
AND USED AS A FIELD GUIDE

STICK FIGURE SYSTEM

High Five/How old are you?/You're big for your age.

Sit at corners of table.

Trace hands.

Draw a PEOPLE.

Identify body parts.

If you don't know the answer, it's OK.

Is it OK for people to touch you on_____?

Did anyone touch you on_____(genitals)?

Who touched you, with what?

Playing a game vs. being mean.

Demo inside vs outside touching.

Break---Truth vs. lies.

Suspects clothes; on/ off.

Penis; erect/non-erect.

Draw size-length of penis. (optional)

Good vs. bad touch.

Secrets. (optional)

Break---Family members, ages etc.

Associated details: day/night, what room, others present,
additional victims, photos, etc.

[CAUTION]
BE SURE TO READ AND UNDERSTAND
THE SFS TEXT BEFORE ATTEMPTING
TO USE THIS OUTLINE

THIS PAGE INTENTIONALLY LEFT BLANK

BIBLIOGRAPHY

Burgess, Ann, R.N., Groth, Dr. Nicholas, Holmstrom, Lynda Lytle and Sgroi, Dr. Suzanne M, *Sexual Assault of Children and Adolescents*, Lexington Books

Forward, Susan and Buck, Craig, *Betrayal of Innocence,* Penquin Books

Rush, Florence, *Sexual Abuse of Children, The Best Kept Secret,* Prentice Hall

Tsang, Daniel, *Age Tabu, (The)*, Slyson Publications

American Psychiatric Association, Anonymous, *Incest Survivors "Open Letter to the Professional Community" and Nightmare of Incest,* Authored by Survivors, ISA, PO Box 5613, Long Beach, CA 90805-0613

Armstrong, Louise, *Kiss Daddy Goodnight,* Hawthorne Books Ind.

Baird, Elizabeth, *I was a Battered Child, Living Books, Tyndale House Publishers*

Brady, Katherine, *Father's Days*, Seaview Books

De Young, Mary, *Sexual Victimization of Children,* McFarland & Company.

Diagnostic and Statistical Manual of Mental Disorders, 3d Edition, Washington D.C.

Dziech, Billy Wright, and Schudson, Charles B, *On Trial-American Courts and their Treatment of Sexually Abused Children,* Beacon Press.

Eberle, Paul & Shirley, *Politics of Child Abuse (The),* Secaucus/Lyle Stuart.

Finkelhor, David, *Sexually Victimized Children,* Free Press

Fox, Robin, *Red Lamp of Incest*, Dutton Publishers

Geiser, Robert, *Hidden Victims-The Sexual Abuse of Children,* Beacon Press

Gil, Elaina Dr., *Outgrowing The Pain,* Launch Press, Box 40174, San Francisco

Goldstein, Seth, *Sexual Exploitation of Children (The) -A Practical Guide to Assessment, Investigation, and Intervention*, Elsevier Service Publishing Co., Inc.

Groth, Nicholas, M.D., and Birnbaum, H. Jean, *Men Who Rape-the Psychology of the Offender.*

Groth, Nicholas, *Child Molester (The),* Social Work and Child Sexual Abuse

Hayden, Torey L *One Child,* Avon Books, G.P. Putnam's Sons.

Herman, Judith Lewis, *Father-Daughter Incest,* Harvard Press

Hollingsworth, Jan, *Unspeakable Acts,* Congdon and Weed Publishers

Irvine, Lucy, *Runaway,* Random House

Janus, Sam, *Death of Innocence (The)*, Morrow Publishing Co.

Justice, Blair and Rita, *Abusing Family,(The),* Human Sciences Press

Justice, Blair and Rita, *Broken Taboo (The), Human Sciences Press*

Keys, Dr. Daniel, *Minds of Billy Mulligan (The),* Random House.

Lenderer, Laura, *Take Back the Night,* Everest House.

Meiselman, Dr. Karin Carlson, *Incest*, Jossey Bess Publishing

Miller, Alice, *Drama of the Gifted Child-The Search for the True Self,* Basic Books

Miller, Alice, *Thou Shalt Not Be Aware,* Basic Books

Morris, Michelle, *If I Should Die Before I Wake,* Tarc Publishers

Rogers, Dale Evans, Mead, Frank S, *Hear the Children Crying, Power Books*

Scriber, Flora Rheta, *Sybil,* Warner Books

Smith, Michelle, and Pazder, Lawrence, M.D., *Michelle Remembers,*. Cogdon & Lottes, Inc.

Spencer, Judith, Suffer the Child, Pocket Books

Van Allen, Charlotte, Daddy's Girl, Simon & Schuster

Walterman, Jill and MacFarland, Kee, *Sexual Abuse of Young Children (The),*. Guilford Press

Weisberg, Kelly, *Children of the Night, Lexington Books.*

Wolbert, Ann Burgess, *Child Pornography and Sex Rings,* Lextington Books.

Woodbury, John Ph D., *Silent Sin (The),* Elroy Schwartz. Signet Books

See Also:

The Accommodation Syndrome, A paper by Dr. Roland Summit. Published in the American Journal of Psychotherapy

Dr. Gene Abel's published statistics on the *"Sexual Perpetrators-Their victimsand their crimes"*. Published by Johns Hopkins Hospital in American Medical Association Journals. (Available at most public libraries-research departments. or through Johns Hopkins Institute.)

The National Center for Missing and Exploited Children (NCMEC) has published and make available several excellent **FREE** reference text books and pamphlets. Be sure to ask when you place your order if you'd like copies in another language; some of their publications are also available in Braille.

Suggested readings:

Analysis: Interviewing Child Victims of Sexual Exploitation and Investigator's Guide.

Children Traumatized in Sex Rings

Child Molesters: A Behavioral Analysis

Just in Case (set). A series of informative brochures on prevention and intervention.

Missing and Abducted Children: A Law Enforcement Guide to Case Investigation.

Sex Rings: A Behavioral Analysis of the Offender.

*Youth at Risk: (*Runaways*)*

Funded by the Office of Juvenile Delinquency and Planning, co-authored by the professionals at NCMEC, experienced FBI officers and other highly qualified individuals, these are "must have" materials for your library and may be obtained by writing to NCMEC, referencing the above titles and sending your request to:

The National Center for Missing and Exploited Children

2201 Wilson Boulevard, Suite 550

Arlington, VA 22201-3502.

If you want to call first and see if they have any "new releases" to add to your request, the phone number is 703-235-3900 or 1-800-The Lost.

List of Illustrations

1. Seating arrangement for interviewing child. (page 29)

2. Hand tracings. (page 30)

3. Stick figure identifying body parts. (page 31)

4. Pre-drawn anatomy "girl." (page 32

5. Pre-drawn anatomy "boy." (page 33)

6. Pre-drawn anatomy "adult female." (page 34)

7. Pre-drawn anatomy "adult male." (page 35)

8. Estimated penis length. (page 36)

9. Use of fingers illustrating vaginal touching. (page 37)

10. Use of finger to illustrate flaccid and erect penis. (page 38)

11. FBI's Pipeline Theory. (page 65)

12. Shift in family structure that leads to incest. (page 67)

We'd like to hear from you!!

Become a part of our voice for the victims. Please take a minute and drop us a line. We'd like to hear your reactions and any suggestions regarding our book.

Have you experienced any success using our simple technique? We'd like to hear about them. Would our technique have produced a different outcome had you known of it?

We'd like to hear other *"potholes in the road to justice"* examples. Send us your own horror stories about molestation or rape cases for possible addition to our next edition. They can be from personal experience at any level of investigation, prosecution, social services or the courts.
We can be contacted at:

LawTech Publishing Co., Ltd.
1060 Calle Cordillera, Ste. 105
San Clemente, CA 92673

(949) 498-4815
Fax: (949) 498-4858
e-mail: lawtech@fia.net